Children's Rights 0–8

Children's Rights 0–8 explores the relevance of children's participatory rights in education, particularly at a time when there are competing demands in meeting the rigid curriculum frameworks whilst taking into account children's entitlement to participate in matters affecting their lives. It engages with theoretical and practical models of participation with an aim to support reflective practice. The chapters are informed by wider academic debates and examples from research and everyday practice in early years settings, making it an accessible read for students and practitioners, as well as researchers.

Mallika Kanyal is Senior Lecturer at Anglia Ruskin University, UK, an institution with a strong reputation for Early Childhood Studies.

Children's Rights 0–8

Promoting participation in education and care

Edited by
Mallika Kanyal

LONDON AND NEW YORK

First published 2014
by Routledge
2 Park Square, Milton Park, Abingdon, Oxon OX14 4RN

and by Routledge
711 Third Avenue, New York, NY 10017

Routledge is an imprint of the Taylor & Francis Group, an informa business

British Library Cataloguing in Publication Data
A catalogue record for this book is available from the British Library

Library of Congress Cataloging in Publication Data
A catalog record for this book has been requested

ISBN: 978-0-415-73572-8 (hbk)
ISBN: 978-1-4082-8596-1 (pbk)
ISBN: 978-1-315-81510-7 (ebk)

Typeset in Bembo and Helvetica Neue
by Florence Production Ltd, Stoodleigh, Devon, UK

Printed and bound in Great Britain by
TJ International Ltd, Padstow, Cornwall

This book is dedicated to the fond memories of my parents, Mr P. S. Negi and Mrs Kusumlata Negi, without whom I wouldn't have had the inspirations to respect children's rights, especially children's participatory rights.

Contents

Children's rights

0–8 years

Overview of the book

The book is a collaborative effort between the members of the Early Childhood Research Group (ECRG) at Anglia Ruskin University and its related allies who work in the field of Early Childhood through education services, such as registered early years settings and pre-schools. The aim of the ECRG is to promote relational pedagogies that invest in learners' experience, be it young children or adults working with them (Early Childhood Research Group, n.d.) We strive to provide a seamless continuum between academia, research and professional practice, evidenced in the work of this book. Most of the work that we do is inspired by the principles of children's agency, well-being and promotion of participatory approaches of working with children and adults.

The book therefore is an attempt to bring not only children's voices but also adults' voices, associated both directly and indirectly with children, directly in their capacity as early years practitioners and indirectly as researchers and academics in the field of Early Childhood. Each group of writers have their own voices and their preferred ways of expressing these voices, written in the form of different chapters. Some parts of the book are written with a strong academic flair and others with a more practical flavour. Chapters are organised not only as a useful academic text but also as narrative case studies giving readers examples of the application of theoretical ideas to everyday practice. The book therefore takes not only a legal but more importantly a relational approach towards our understanding of children's rights, originating from the 'relational pedagogy' strand of the ECRG at the University. It reinstates our belief in the ways in which adults form relationships with children; a relationship of trust, understanding and acceptance which allows the children to express themselves freely (Alin, 2012: 126).

The relationships are explored from a participatory perspective, inspired from the right to Participation of the United Nations Convention on the Rights of the Child (UNCRC, 1989). These rights, broadly speaking, can be categorised into three Ps – the right to **P**articipation, the right to **P**rovision (of services) and the right to **P**rotection. The UNCRC (United Nations, 1989) explains these three Ps in the form of a series of 54 articles, amongst which Article 12 relates to participatory rights. It predicates children's participation and active involvement in processes and decisions that affect their lives, amongst which we believe education and care is an important one. The book, therefore, focuses primarily on children's participation (the first P), but from a relational perspective, making it an accessible and meaningful read for the professionals and students studying Early Childhood and/or Children's Rights. Academic discourses are supported and complemented with examples of children's participation in everyday practice in education and care settings (including early years settings and primary schools). These examples are largely drawn from local settings in the south east of England and also from a school in north India, to which an author has professional alliance. The international perspective, though not the main focus of this book, is used to illustrate sensitivities and complexities involved in implementing a Universal concept (children's rights) across different cultures and practices. The standardisation of a universally constructed but socially interpreted concept raises various issues, ranging from politics to education, some of which are addressed in this book.

The impetus for discussion is drawn from the notion of 'culture of participation' and 'guided participation', concepts we regard as central to the understanding of children's participatory work, explained further in the following chapters. They acknowledge the inclusiveness required in the implementation of children's rights – which can be realised by *not* alienating adults' voices and expertise, but by using them as guidance and support. Emphasis is placed on the need to adopt a holistic approach towards revising our expertise as early childhood practitioners, a role which is not only confined to the knowledge gained by studying developmental psychology but also informed by the principles of new sociology of childhood.

The book is divided into three parts. These three parts are further divided into seven chapters, each written as an individual unit, intended to give readers a choice of being able to dip in and out of the book as appropriate.

Part I starts with the history of childhood and children's rights in Chapters 1 and 2. Chapter 1 gives a historic overview of rights, showing the development of the universal concept from a well-being and social justice perspective. It identifies how issues framing children's rights appear to overlap with humanitarian and political concerns about child welfare. The role played by the international organisations (particularly United Nations ones), such as the United Nations Convention on the Rights of the Child (UNCRC) and United Nations Children's Fund (UNICEF), in promoting children's rights is discussed. Chapter 2 outlines the history of childhood and the contribution of various academic disciplines and the children's rights movement in the conceptualisation of childhood. The social construction of childhood and children's participation is theorised and analysed using a cultural-historical perspective. The pedagogical value of adopting a rights-based approach in education is discussed using a case study example from a local setting in south east England.

Part II explores the relevance of participation in the context of practice. It develops the central theme of relationships by engaging with literature and case study examples in Chapters 3, 4, 5 and 6. Chapter 3 identifies the benefits and challenges of participation, especially by exploring its application in pedagogical practice. It makes reference to understanding participation from a children's behaviour perspective and proposes a 'Spiral of Empowerment' to identify and encourage opportunities for participation. The chapter considers the complex realities of realising participation for all children, including the ones who may choose to stay silent. Chapter 4 introduces, describes and critiques a range of participation models which can be applied within education and care contexts. It explores the role of theoretical and practical models and how they can support pedagogical practice. Ideas are reinforced with the help of case studies and summarised with a discussion on reflexive practice that regards adults as co-constructors in children's worlds. Chapter 5 focuses more on the 'care' aspect of children's development. It discusses issues in relation to the participation of the very young, before they are capable of communicating their ideas through speech. A multi-directional triangle of relationships between parents, practitioners and babies and toddlers is explored, emphasising the role of five Cs: child; curriculum; care; connectedness; and community, in promoting participation. Chapter 6 takes the above discussion further and focuses on the integration of the Early Years Foundation Stage (EYFS) with children's agency and participation by sharing implementation of participatory approaches in two thriving pre-schools. The chapter recognises how children can achieve empowerment when they are listened to and heard through their preferred voice.

Part III explores the use of participatory research approaches in education, especially in early years. It is written as one big chapter, but divided into a further six sections, with a common focus on research. It includes an introduction to participatory research and various traditional and contemporary research methods that could be used as participatory approaches in pedagogical research. The use of children's drawings, interviews, questionnaires, video and aural technology and observations are discussed with examples from the authors' own researches to illustrate the methods being discussed. A detailed discussion on participatory research is outside the scope of this book, but reference is made to the origin, philosophy, ethics and critique of participatory research. The aim is to give the reader examples from research that could be developed as pedagogical approaches and/or research methods to work and research with young children. The application of these methods is analysed using a children's rights framework, recognising and reinstating the value of children's participation in education and care, which is the main focus of this book.

References

Alin, R. 2012. Teaching linear measurement in the Israeli kindergarten curriculum, in T. Papatheodorou and J. Moyles (eds). *Cross-cultural Perspectives on Early Childhood*. London: Sage.

Early Childhood Research Group. n.d. Anglia Ruskin University. [Online]. Available at http://www.aru.ac.uk/ruskin/en/home/microsites/early_childhood_research_group.html. Accessed November 10, 2011.

United Nations. 1989. United Nations Convention on the Rights of the Child. [Online]. Available at http://www.unicef.org/rightsite/237_202.htm. Accessed February 10, 2012.

Acknowledgements

I would like to extend my thanks to all the authors in this volume for their contribution as well as for providing critical feedback to each other in the development of various chapters. I would also like to thank the anonymous reviewers of the proposal and chapters for providing constructive feedback and support for this publication. A special thanks to the staff and children of Saplings Nursery in Henham, Bishop's Stortford, Hertfordshire; Richmond Pre-school, Benfleet, Essex; Absolute Angels Montessori Nursery, Coggeshall, Essex; Solid Start Day Nursery, Chelmsford, Essex; and the school in India, who wholeheartedly embraced the idea of children's participatory rights and allowed us to use examples from their everyday practice.

I would also like to thank Essex County Council for giving us permission to use the revised Early Years Foundation Stage (REYFS) graphic illustration in Chapter 4.

Last, but not least, I would like to acknowledge and thank our Masters and Undergraduate student researchers who contributed in the form of case studies and children's observations. Special thanks to Sarah Thackeray, Rugina Begum, Amal Hussein and Opeyemi Osadiya, from the Department of Education, Anglia Ruskin University.

Mallika Kanyal

Acknowledgements

Introduction

Mallika Kanyal

Rights can be considered from a legal, social justice and relationship perspective. The United Nations Convention on the Rights of the Child (UNCRC, 1989) is a political treaty where governments strive to implement the articles they have ratified by being a signatory to the international convention. Implementation is through national and/or regional laws and policies which govern the childhood experiences within their political domain. The governance can be established through services in education, care and social care sector where professionals are regulated to act in certain ways in order to achieve the pre-established targets. The understanding of 'rights' from this perspective can yield a very deficit view of childhood where children's entitlements can be portrayed merely at a tokenistic level in order to conform to adult dominated agendas to standardised performivity. The whole concept of universalisation and standardisation can be perceived to be challenging the professional roles and responsibilities where people's creativity may be compromised due to the developing culture of compliance in the workplace.

This book is an attempt to understand rights from a 'relationship' perspective and how despite living in a world of 'contract' and 'services' we strive to provide enabling environments to young children within early years settings. The focus of the book is around children's participation, which according to the UNCRC, entitles children to express their views in all matters affecting their lives (Article 12) through various forms of expression (Article 13), including oral, writing or in print, in the form of art, or through any other media of the child's choice (United Nations, 1989). These rights are made more specific for early years through the 'General Comment No. 7', published by the UN Committee on the Rights of the Child in 2005. Early childhood, according to this committee, includes all young children – from birth and throughout infancy; during the preschool years; as well as during the transition to school (UN Committee on the Rights of the Child, 2005).

The scope of children's participatory rights is vast and has been realised in various aspects of life, for example education, medical, social care and social justice, but to define participation within the scope of this book, we are considering participation from a relationship perspective within early years settings. The aim is to consider various ways through which relationships between children and adults can be strengthened by not only empowering children but also developing a shared understanding between adults and children about their needs, perspectives and experiences.

Children's participation has primarily been addressed through programmes and researches involving 'children's voices'. The concept of children's voices can be associated with the New Sociology of Childhood discipline which aims to develop a better understanding of childhood considering their perspectives. The prime aim of the work around children's voice agenda was initially to represent the socially disempowered position of childhood to the world and consider issues not only from a legal and social justice perspective but also from a moral perspective (human activist perspective). Its use has now broadened and has gradually taken the shape of 'good practice' where knowledge is believed to be developed in collaboration with the 'local experts'. In education and care settings its potential is realised in various forms, for example through schools' councils, children's participation in documenting their own learning, children's participation in constructing their own learning environments and various other processes. However, in any work involving children, their participation must be viewed critically. The role children play in such work can range from researchers to participants and through any published work it is essential that we consider the explicit or implicit image we give of children by representing their voices.

Like any other right within the UNCRC, participation is also a socially constructed right, the conceptualisation of which is influenced by the everyday practices, values and behaviours that we, as a social group, uphold and believe in. The chapters in this book therefore acknowledge the situated nature of childhood and the authors are aware of the scope, possibility and limitation of participatory approaches. Like any other (research) methods, they may not always represent social reality, as the methods we choose to understand children's perspectives can have institutional or researcher bias. Voices, therefore, should not be regarded as individual, fixed, straightforward, linear or clear, but instead as a socially co-constructed concept (Komulainen, 2007: 18, 23) which can be shaped by multiple factors such as our own assumptions about children, our particular use of language, the institutional contexts in which we operate and the overall ideological and discursive climates which prevail (Spyrou, 2011).

Children's voices, from a multiple perspective (children, practitioner and researcher) can, however, offer a useful framework to developing a shared understanding of children's experiences where children are at the heart and centre of practice, and their voices are attended by adults around them. Listening, thereafter, should be regarded reflexively to include interpretation, meaning making and responding (Clark et al., 2003), a process which has both transformative and empowering potential.

Realising this from a pedagogic position, the UNCRC, in particular children's right to participation, can have various implications on the role of education and care professionals. Some of these are summarised as below:

- It challenges the traditional role of practitioners and urges us to change the way we think about ourselves as adults (Woodhead, 2005). In order to support this change early years professionals need to consider and redefine their expertise (MacNaughton, 2007) in line with the New Sociology of Childhood, the principles of which are not solely based on Developmental Psychology but also on how children view themselves as social actors and participants.
- Adoption of participatory processes in everyday practice leads to outcomes for both children and adults. It is not only children who feel empowered by being listened to but adults too. Adults invariably enter into a reflexive process, where they become co-learners and co-interpreters (Mannion, 2010), making it a mutual and worthwhile experience. Engagement with such processes may urge the practitioners to challenge the dominant discourses of meaning making and evolve their own philosophy of care and education, informed by their interaction with children and other adults in the setting (Dahlberg et al., 2006).
- With the changing ideas of childhood, sometimes we may ignore their vulnerable side. In order to deliver the best practice, practitioners must therefore recognise children as both competent and vulnerable and dependent (Kjørholt, 2008), respecting the multiple ways in which they may choose to express themselves, be it vocal, through an artefact or their silence.
- The caveat of rights is that they should be considered from a broader and holistic perspective and not as a precursor to developing individual, self-centred children. Its paramount role is to ensure the well-being of children, which can be achieved by balancing different rights so that they function in the best interests of children. The right to participation cannot be understood in isolation from other articles: for example, Article 12, as a general principle, is linked to the other general principles of the Convention, such as Article 2 (the right to non-discrimination), Article 6 (the right to life, survival and development) and, in particular, is interdependent with Article 3 (primary consideration of the best interests of the child). The article is also closely linked with the articles related to civil rights and freedoms, particularly Article 13 (the right to freedom of expression) and Article 17 (the right to information) (Bae, 2010: 207).

This brings us to the summary, where I would like to reinstate the importance of relational pedagogy in which we are trying to situate participatory rights. It goes back to the principles of 'connectedness', 'interaction' and 'relationships', the aspects of pedagogy which can be honed by the application of participatory approaches (Papatheodorou, 2010). Relational pedagogy supports the building of a supportive learning environment which is rich in trust, understanding and acceptance, and which enables the children to express themselves freely (Alin, 2012: 126). The following chapters are an endeavour to open up the debate on children's participation, referring to both its possibilities and challenges and at the same time showcasing some examples from everyday practice and research.

References

Alin, R. 2012. Teaching linear measurement in the Israeli kindergarten curriculum, in T. Papatheodorou and J. Moyles (eds). *Cross-cultural Perspectives on Early Childhood.* London: Sage.

Bae, B. 2010. Realising children's right to participation in early childhood settings: some critical issues in a Norwegian context. *Early Years*, 30 (3): 205–218.

Clark, A., McQuail, S. and Moss, P. 2003. Exploring the field of listening to and consulting with young children. *Research Report* 445. London: Department for Education and Skills.

Dahlberg, G., Moss, P. and Pence, A. 2006. Pedagogical documentation: A practice for reflection and democracy, in *Beyond Quality in Early Childhood Education.* London: Routledge.

Kjørholt, A. T. 2008. Children as new citizens: in the best interests of the child? in A. James and A. James, (eds). *European Childhoods: Cultures, Politics and Childhoods in Europe.* Chippenham: Palgave Macmillan.

Komulainen, S. 2007. The ambiguity of the child's 'voice' in social research. *Childhood*, 14(1): 11–28.

MacNaughton, G. 2007. Early childhood professionals and children's rights: tensions and possibilities around the United Nations General Comment No. 7 on Children's Rights. *International Journal of Early Years Education*, 15 (2): 161–170.

Mannion, G. 2010. After participation: the socio-spatial performance of intergenerational becoming, in B. Percy-Smith and N. Thomas (eds). *A Handbook of Children and Young People's Participation: Perspectives from Theory and Practice.* London and New York: Routledge.

Papatheodorou, T. 2010. The pedagogy of playful learning environments, in J. Moyles (ed.). *Thinking about Play: Developing a Reflective Approach.* Maidenhead: Open University Press.

Spyrou, S. 2011. The limits of children's voices: from authenticity to critical, reflexive representation. *Childhood*, 18(2): 151–165.

United Nations. 1989. United Nations Convention on the Rights of the Child. [Online]. Available at http://www.unicef.org/rightsite/237_202.htm. Accessed February 10, 2012.

UN Committee on the Rights of the Child. 2005. General Comment No. 7: Implementing Child Rights in Early Childhood. [Online]. Available at http://www2.ohchr.org/english/bodies/crc/docs/AdvanceVersions/GeneralComment7Rev1.pdf. Accessed February 10, 2012.

Woodhead, M. 2005. Early childhood development: a question of rights. *International Journal of Early Childhood*, 37 (3): 79–98.

PART

Childhood and children's rights

CHAPTER

History and development of children's rights

Christine Such

Aims of the chapter

1. To outline the history of children's rights, with a focus on the implementation of the United Nations Convention on the Rights of the Child (UNCRC, 1989) and its role in promoting the rights of the child.
2. To identify how issues framing children's rights appear to overlap with humanitarian and political concerns about child welfare.
3. To consider why recognition of children's participation is important in shaping the present agenda on the rights of the child, and the advancement of children as political selves.

Introduction

This chapter examines the history of children's rights by identifying issues which are woven into child welfare. It will show how concerns about the state of childhood emerged to influence the creation of UNCRC, 1989. The first part of the chapter examines themes in child welfare which shaped the passage of UNCRC, 1989. The Convention, for example, is significant because of how it positions the child, both as subject, and as the object of rights, which has implications for child welfare and children's well-being (Tomas, 2008). The second part of the chapter explores the role of UNCRC to reveal why a more child-centred approach to the study of childhood and children's welfare emerged (Hagglund and Thelander, 2011). Such an open approach to working with children encourages practitioners to use participatory strategies which position the children, even the young child, as active and competent beings (MacNaughton et al., 2007; Papatheodorou and Moyles, 2009). These approaches to children's welfare have parallels with research, and to the study of childhood, in which the child is participant and subject of their world (Alanen, 2011;

James, 2010). James (2010) argues for the need to research children's daily lives and to consider not only what sets children's lives apart from adults but also to contextualise these experiences. In part this approach shows why adult voices, especially those of parents and professionals, have dominated debates on children's rights. A theme throughout this book is how children's rights to participation shape current professional practice, and understanding of their everyday lives. Later chapters in this book explore these themes in more detail.

Rights – what rights?

There is a special quality to children's rights which Tomas (2008) identifies when she describes children as being both the subject and object of rights. To be the object of rights stresses children's dependent status, and reliance on adults to meet children's welfare. Three different models are used by MacNaughton, Hughes and Smith (2007) to represent the young child in relation to adults in policy making in the Western world. The models are useful in showing the genesis of adult control and how it operates to contain, and even deny, children's engagement in decision making. For example, in the first model, MacNaughton et al. (2007) show how the young child is treated as a possession of adults who mould appropriate behaviours. In the second model, the child is subject to adult control in order to protect children's innocence and foster their development. The final model accepts the child as participant yet only able to act when they are deemed by adults as sufficiently competent to do so. The idea of the child as participant represents the child as subject of rights. The three models provide a useful framework to show how adult control constrains young children's participation in policy making. One way of exploring these different aspects which I have used in my own teaching is by asking students to create a wish list of children's rights and then rank their importance, as shown in Box 1.1: Making a 'wish' list of children's rights.

Furthermore, Ennew (2008) explains why notions of children's citizenship need to be developed to appreciate children's involvement and here she offers an alternative view of why children's participation is limited by adult authority. She shows how within the aegis of the United Nations children's involvement in meetings about children's rights is limited by adults. Wall (2011: 92) identifies why 'political spaces in which children are empowered to express their own distinctive and submerged points of views' are necessary to encourage children's inclusion. What is important is that children have space to express their views, and for adults to listen and respect these views, and take seriously children's involvement (MacNaughton et al., 2007). Thus the nature of the relationship between children, their parents and wider adult society is important to understanding children's rights and why recognition of rights to protection dominates rights to participation.

BOX 1.1: MAKING A 'WISH' LIST OF CHILDREN'S RIGHTS

Make a list of rights which children should have. List at least ***five*** different ideas.

1. With a partner share your ideas and decide which rights are the most important and place them in order of importance. As you decide on your priorities share your reasons. Compile your list and be prepared to share.
2. Each pair of students will present one idea starting with their first priority.
3. As each pair shares their ideas a list will be made and priorities will be shown. At the end a final list will be produced by the class.

By sharing their ideas and listing rights in order of priority students will debate which rights are important to children's lives and why. Students readily identify young children's need to be protected from abuse, and explain its importance to child welfare and to professional concerns about the nature of childhood. Few students cite the need for young children's rights to participation and when they do these rights are listed below rights of protection.

The exercise is useful because it raises further questions about the nature of human rights in general and the issues affecting children's rights, and if they are rights holders (Franklin, 1995, 2002; Fortin, 2008; MacNaughton et al., 2007; Milne, 2008; and Ennew, 2008).

Alanen (2011: 147) encourages students, and professionals working with children, to question existing social practices to reveal how 'children's lives are organised and regulated, and childhood undervalued in modern societies'. Only then can alternative strategies which promote a better life for children emerge. She recognises that for this work to flourish children's perspectives need to be presented as part of the process of claims-making. Reynolds, Nieuwenhuys and Hanson (2006) present a persuasive case for children's inclusion using methods of ethnography of childhood to capture children's perspectives. Johansson (2011) reveals how the (adult) researcher becomes 'co-producer' with children in ethnographic studies of children's lives, which opens up questions about the nature of these research relationships. In the next section the rights granted to children under UNCRC, 1989 are explored and the nature of relationships between children and adults is examined.

UNCRC, 1989 and why it is special

Children have been described as the last group in society to be granted access to rights, long after adult suffrage (Franklin, 1995, 2002). Childhood is seen as a passing phase, so that rights denied to us when we are young are ours to claim in our adult years. At what point we make this transition and become full rights holders will differ between societies and across the generations.

The UNCRC, 1989 is special because it presents a watershed in establishing a rights framework for children which includes their right to participation. The rights set out in UNCRC cover economic, social, cultural, civil and political rights for children, aged 18 or less (Jones, 2011). When it was passed, this Convention was critical to establishing agreement between countries on the rights granted to children to improve their lives. The Convention includes a number of specific articles which include children's rights to provision of services, their rights to protection and to participation in society. Significantly, Black (1996: 1) describes how 'children's emergence as a topic of public and political concern has been striking. At national and international levels, leaders in all parts of the world have begun to identify themselves with family and children's issues'.

Franklin (1995, 2002) provides a useful perspective on children's rights by differentiating between legal, moral, welfare and liberty rights to appreciate the status of children's rights. It helps to explain the special position of children vis-à-vis adults. Legal rights are rights which can be enforced by law and which are written, for example the right to education. Here the emphasis is on setting clear objectives which can be monitored and their outcomes evaluated. Kaufman and Rizzini (2009: 425) argue that 'legal norms can become powerful tools in advocacy by national, as well as international organisations on behalf of children' which contribute to changing attitudes and actions. Welfare rights, for example the right to shelter, appear more concrete because they are linked to the principle of acting in the *best interests of the child* to promote their well-being. It is a principle which underpins child and family welfare and is directly linked to the need to provide child protection. In contrast moral rights, for example children's right to express a choice, or young children's right to play, are rights we aspire to, and which we claim as inspirational goals to achieve. Often it is adults who make these claims on behalf of children. They are more elusive because they depend on what society values. Equally, liberty rights, such as the right to participate in decision making, for example the right to vote, appear more illusionary for children. Children's rights to participation and involvement are presented either as unnecessary or as a step too far because it challenges adult authority.

Children's dependency on their parents limits their status as rights holders. Ultimately it is parents who take responsibility for their children and exercise a duty of care. Thus children's welfare and their rights can only be realised through parents and other adults (Roche, 1999). Franklin's (1995, 2002) work highlights the difficulties of challenging adult authority to address children's rights. The tensions shown in Figure 1.1 between children's rights and parental rights reveal that children's perceived lack of competency and agency reinforce their dependency on others. The strain between children's and parents' rights is difficult to reconcile because the nature of these relationships is bounded by ties of intimacy and care (Johansson, 2011). Gittins (1998) traces the idea of children's dependency on others, especially to their parents, with the notion that children belong to their parents and are their 'property' and thus a private concern. She shows how these ideas frame legal and economic relationships between parent and child. Underlying these relationships are the perceived differences between adults and children, in terms of knowledge, experience and power. Children's lack of competency and their immaturity is compared unfavourably to adults (Freeman, 1995, 2000). Freeman (2009) identifies problems of interpretation and ambiguity surrounding the issues illustrated in Figure 1.1. The tensions highlight philosophical questions about societal views of childhood and why children's dependency on others limits their freedom to act (Gittins, 1998; Roche, 1999; Johansson, 2011). The child lacks experience of the world, and the necessary autonomy to act in their own self-interest. Johansson (2011) explains why children's dependency on adults frames ideas about the nature of the relationship between parent and child, and these also shape ideas on child welfare.

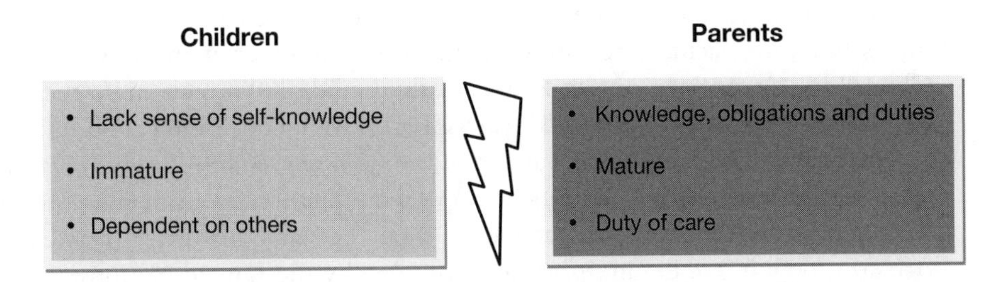

FIGURE 1.1 Tensions exist between children's rights and parental rights

Children's right to participation lags behind their right to protection from abuse. One reason for this is because giving children a voice, and the right to have a say about what happens to them, involves recognition of children's agency and self-knowledge. Critical to these considerations is how actively adults appreciate children's competency and ability to express themselves, and their willingness to engage with children in open dialogue (Davies and Artaraz, 2009). However, perceptions of children's competency are bounded by age, yet recognition of the value of using democratic practices may overcome these boundaries.

In later chapters the nature of the relationship between early years practitioners and the children they work with is examined. The practical strategies which practitioners employ to engage young children's participation in daily routines is explored and shows recognition of children's agency and self-knowledge (MacNaughton et al., 2007; Davies and Artaraz, 2009). The importance of these strategies is how well they reveal ways of working with young children to capture their engagement as active partners in daily routines. In order for *all* children to realise that they are considered and listened to, adults in an education context should 'build a rapport' with children and 'provide feedback' in a clear and age appropriate way (DfES, 2005). Providing feedback can entail repeating or commenting on what the children say or have expressed, in order to engage with them, whilst also letting them know they have been heard, listened to and understood with the intention of acting on it (Davies and Artaraz, 2009).

Children's rights and child-centred welfare

The UNCRC is the first legally binding international instrument to incorporate the full range of human rights – civil, cultural, economic, political and social rights (Kaufman and Rizzini, 2009). It is intended to establish rights for all children and young people aged less than 18 years. The articles in the Convention cover: provision of services for children; child protection; and children's rights to participation, as shown in Box 1.2.

Children's participation rights (Box 1.2) are important as they provide the touchstone for creating child-centred welfare. A key consideration of Article 12 concerns ideas about children's competence to participate and at what age this is likely to occur. The United Nations Committee on the Rights of the Child (UN Committee on the Rights of the Child, 2005) recognised the need to clarify the wording of Article 12 (UNCRC, 1989), concerning children's 'age and maturity'. The committee stated that the '*youngest children's*' rights regarding their views and feelings should be respected; therefore consideration should be given to *all* children irrespective of their 'age and maturity' (Davies and Artaraz, 2009: 57). The interpretation provided by the United Nations General Comment No. 7 on UNCRC was important because it provides a quasi legal document to identify actions required by governments to ensure its implementation and also its recognition in early years. More recently, guidance has been sought on Article 31 which covers children's right 'to rest and leisure, to engage in play and recreational activities appropriate to the age of the child and

BOX 1.2: UNCRC, 1989 – KEY PROVISIONS

Provision Articles recognise the social rights of children to minimum standards of health, education, social security, physical care, family life, play, recreation, culture and leisure.

Protection Articles identify the rights of children to be safe from discrimination, physical and sexual abuse, exploitation, substance abuse, injustice and conflict.

Participation Articles are about civil and political rights. The rights of children to a name and identity, to be consulted and to be taken account of, to access information, to freedom of speech and opinion, and to challenge decisions made on their behalf. Article 12 in the Convention outlines children's rights in relation to participation; it states that all children capable of formulating their own judgement have the right to express their opinion on the subjects that affect them.

to participate freely in cultural life and the arts' (CRAE's summary of the Convention on the Rights of the Child, n.d.). The focus on play is of special interest to children and to the expression of their interests which is covered in later chapters in this book.

There clearly is a relationship between different aspects of rights in the Convention, which is illustrated in Figure 1.2.

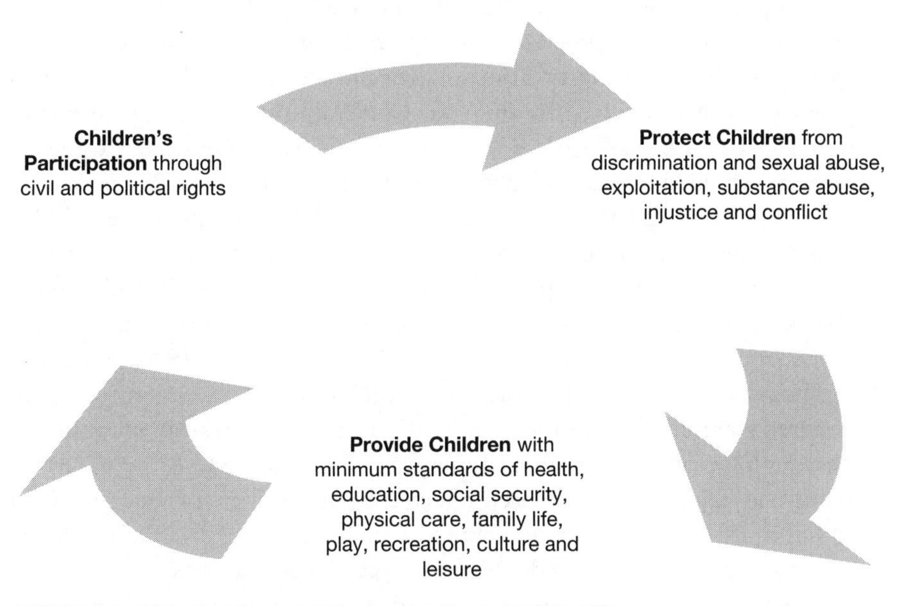

FIGURE 1.2 Children's rights and child-centred welfare in UNCRC, 1989

There are different understandings of childhood between societies and to some extent it is these which constrain the scope of the Convention and limit child welfare (Freeman, 2009). These social constructions of childhood may help us to understand why in the West we adopt very different approaches to children's labour compared to the developing world (Wall, 2011). But whose standards are correct? And can we ever achieve a universal standard for childhood? Perhaps the answers to these questions are not straightforward, yet a comparative approach to children's lives based on examining the contexts, and reality of children's experiences, may provide some answers (Alanen, 2011).

Global approaches to children's rights: past and present

The relationship between rights and welfare centres on concerns about the needs of children and state of childhood. One early example of these links was the launch of the Save the Children Fund, by Dorothy Buxton in 1919, to raise funds for children affected by war throughout Europe (Milne, 2008). Buxton had the active support of her sister Eglantyne Jebb who made a significant contribution to drafting a 'Children's Charter', later adopted by the League of Nations in 1924. The Charter was important in establishing children's rights as an international issue. The 'children's movement' in the twentieth century highlighted the special needs of children and their vulnerability, especially in times of war, and why concerns about child protection dominated social welfare (Stainton Rogers, 2001; Hagglund and Thelander, 2011; Hoffman, 2012). The theme of war and catastrophe continues to resonate with the imagery of the vulnerable child, and perhaps explains why protection is uppermost in child welfare. Cheney (2010) examines why international humanitarian intervention in Africa focuses on the plight of orphans affected by the Aids pandemic. She compares interventionist strategies based on child protection with rights-based approaches using welfare services which transform all children's lives. Hoffman (2012) goes further to show how representations of children's vulnerability dominate the aid agencies' strategies of child rescue and argues this explains why protectionism persists.

Unicef continues to play an important role in global children's rights (Black, 1996; Knutsson, 1997; Kaufman and Rizzini, 2009). The organisation was created by the UN General Assembly in December 1946, in response to the humanitarian crisis following the Second World War, and in recognition of children's suffering as a consequence (Black, 1996). It was named as the United Nations International Children's Emergency Fund (Unicef). Although its original remit had been to help children affected by the war in Europe and China, it stayed in existence to provide help to all children whose lives were plighted by poverty throughout the world. Unicef was granted permanent status by the General Assembly in 1953, and continues to provide relief, services and support for children (Black, 1996).

There are four important phases in the agency's history which show how its work with children has been approached. They include: emergency-humanitarian relief; developing the child; basic services strategy; and the final one based on rights of the child (Knutsson, 1997). The different approaches are still present in child welfare and suggest that rights are framed by concerns over children's needs and the state of childhood. In summary a rights-based approach is based on the principle of 'in the best interests of the child' and how this is addressed creates different welfare strategies illustrated in the phases of development of Unicef.

Emergency-humanitarian relief

Both Black (1996) and Knutsson (1997) cover the early history of Unicef through the lives of those who played a key role in developing the work of this agency. Theirs is an important contribution, and their stories help to explain why recognition of children's rights as a human rights issue was protracted. The first international agreement on children's rights was in 1924 with the adoption by the League of Nations of the World Child Welfare Charter. The ideas behind this approach were based on the work of the voluntary Save the Children movement and through its work with poor children (Milne, 2008). The Charter identified five key principles: 'the child's right to material, moral and spiritual development; to special help when hungry, sick, disabled or orphaned; to first call on relief in distress; not to be economically exploited; and to an upbringing that instilled a sense of responsibility towards society' (Black, 1996: 21).

The notion of concern for children, as an organising principle of knowledge about the condition of children, is important to the development of children's rights. The basis of philanthropic action is emergency-humanitarian relief. At its heart is a willingness by society to take action based on collective concern for children in need. At times it is the numbers of children whose lives are blighted, and the sheer size of a problem affecting children's survival, health and well-being, which appear critical to raising awareness (Cheney, 2010; Hagglund and Thelander, 2011; Hoffman, 2012). Yet, increasingly, it is the human story behind these numbers which unmasks the reality of children's lives, which provokes a response from the public. Representations and media images of children's suffering encourage action by society through government and voluntary movements acting on behalf of children to improve their welfare (Burman, 2008; Cheney, 2010; Hoffman, 2012). The role of charity is twofold: to provide relief and to campaign for change to improve the quality of children's lives. Therborn (1996) describes how movements such as Save the Children exposed the absence of support for children of the 'defeated enemy' in the 1900s: the needs of these children were being ignored and their plight worsened by the absence of community, and international support. The role of charities has expanded and they continue to shape national and international developments in support of children's welfare (Burman, 2008; Cheney, 2010; Penn, 2011). Burman (2008) examines the descriptions of development and argues there is a parallel between representations of development from children to adults, with development of richer and poorer countries. By focusing on the parallel between these two, Burman (2008: 188) emphasises the ways in which 'poverty, deficit, and dependence' are reinforced to present children in poorer countries as innocent victims.

Developing the child

From the 1950s onwards Unicef began to focus its work on concern for the whole child and provision of local services to promote children's physical and intellectual development (Knutsson, 1997). This work represents important social investment in childhood and has been shown to make a difference in children's lives. McDowell and Lyons (2009) have shown how programmes supporting children's holistic development can, and do, make a positive difference in young children's lives. Heckman (2000, cited in Penn, 2011) has shown how investment in early childhood education and care programmes helps to maximise children's potential and provide returns which compare favourably to later stages of education and schooling. This human capital theory has been used in recent years to promote the use of early childhood education and care programmes in the developing world (Penn, 2011). It is a powerful argument as it resonates with seeing the child as a project, but rather than focus on the child's suffering it is their potential which is the focus of action. There are limitations to this approach which is based on Western theories of children's normative development, and programmes using these perspectives may ignore the social and cultural realities of children's lives in the developing world (Cheney, 2010; Penn, 2011).

Knutsson (1997) identified the limitations of using local initiatives in the 1950s as the schemes were dominated by outsiders, Western experts, who did not always engage with local communities to create sustainable provision. It is a fault line observed in the use of aid programmes whose success requires governments and funders to work across boundaries between health, care and education in delivery of services (Penn, 2011). Only by working across boundaries will services begin to flourish to establish a sense of permanency, and with this sustainability of provision. Knutsson (1997) is passionate about the need to include children's services within economic development if a future for all children is to be secured. Burman (2008) argues that development is not a singular concept because child development and ideas of growth and progress are linked to ideas about economic development. Thus she describes developments (emphasis on the plural) as important to understanding children's welfare. Heckman (2000, cited in Penn, 2011), for example, focuses on the economic returns gained from the Perry HighScope projects in the USA as evidence of successful early intervention. The link between investment in early childhood education and outcomes is critical to political support provided by governments for early intervention programmes (Papatheodorou and Moyles, 2012). In contrast Knutsson's (1997) claims are based on the importance of including children's active participation. Children should not be the passive recipients but active subjects of child welfare strategies. Alanen (2011: 147) echoes these values when she writes of the critical importance of 'listening to children and conveying their perspectives into the knowledge of the state of childhood' because their voices will 'help in improving the social standing of children and childhood in social life, and to enhance children's well-being in their actual everyday circumstances'.

Basic services strategy

In the 1960s the developing child approach was revised so that a basic services strategy was adopted by Unicef. Central to this approach was the recognition of the need for reliable long-term funding to promote an effective local infrastructure to provide health, education and welfare for all. Only when these basic services existed would child welfare become reality for all children.

Rights of the child strategy

This is the last phase of development leading to the creation and adoption of UNCRC, 1989. In the late 1970s the emphasis on the rights of the child began to emerge as a way of advocating for children's welfare. It was established on the principle that children and young people need special protection from exploitation; the right to develop to their fullest potential; and to participate fully in family, cultural and social life. It is the use of the rights of the child strategy with the focus on participation which is central to the discussion throughout chapters of this book. When the Convention was passed there were 60 signatories immediately and within ten months it came into force (Freeman, 2000). By agreeing to undertake the obligations in the Convention governments commit themselves to protecting and ensuring children's rights, and to be held accountable for meeting their obligations.

Freeman (2009) describes the issues which caused tension between the different nations as they debated and then agreed the terms of the Convention. These included: Article 14 on freedom of thought, conscience and religion, adoption, rights of the unborn child, traditional practices such as Female Genital Mutilation (FGM), and the duty to respect and provide for parents. The differences between states showed how traditional approaches to childhood contain the scope of universal action. It has to be noted that there was no evidence of children or children's groups being asked about their approach to children's rights. Only much later were the rights of very young children identified as a group project and Woodhead (2008) explains why this occurred in 2004–5. When we look at the issues raised here our gaze begins to shift more to parental responsibilities and the actions of early childhood professionals. It is the institutionalisation of childhood which is the focus.

Providing for children's welfare and well-being

For children to be seen to have rights there needs to be a willingness to recognise that action can be taken to improve their well-being (Franklin, 1995, 2002; Freeman, 2009). Figure 1.3 shows how providing humanitarian relief performs an essential role for children's survival and welfare. However, in the absence of a basic service strategy to ensure sustainability of provision the future for all children may continue to be bleak. Therborn (1996) describes the process of claims-making – that is, by showing the unmet needs of children, we can legitimise the condition of childhood as a cause for concern, requiring intervention. Davidson (2011), for example, illustrates the difficulties faced by refugee and migrant children compared with trafficked children. In theory all these children have universal rights to welfare yet in practice access to services is limited and politically contested. She contrasts societies' willingness to intervene and 'free trafficked children from their snare' (Davidson, 2011: 472) compared to refugee and migrant children whose suffering is compounded by immigration policy and its enforcement.

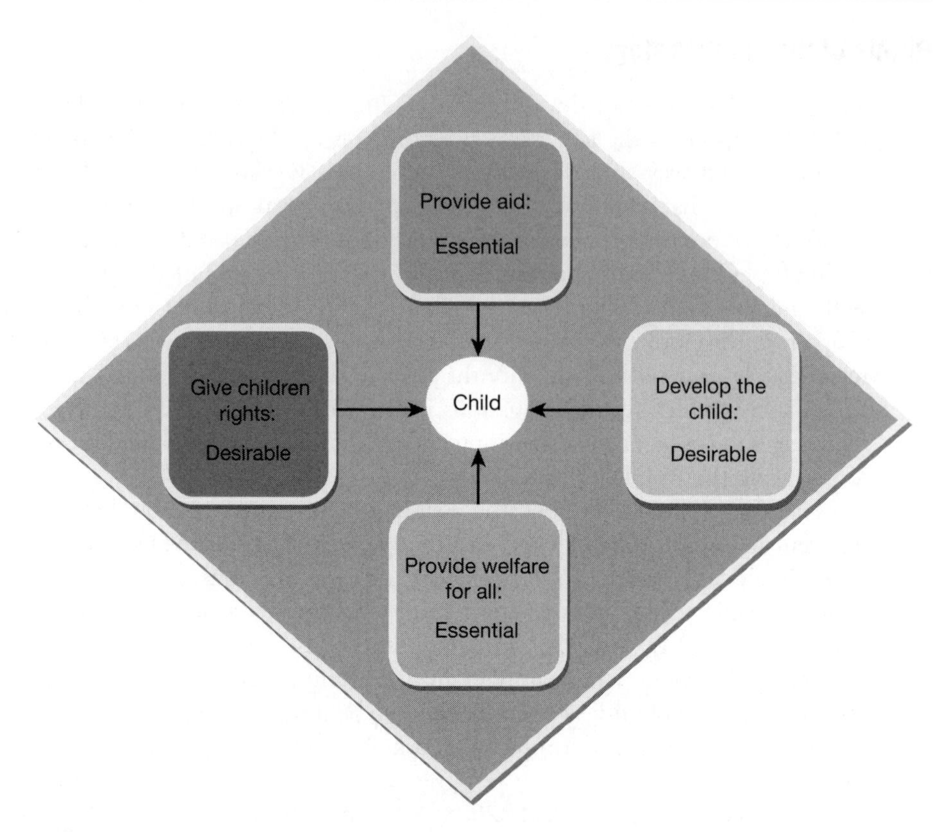

FIGURE 1.3 Providing for children's welfare: action and concerns

The idea of claims-making helps to show the contested nature of representations of concerns about children's lives. Cheney (2010) illustrates how international aid agencies in their desire to improve the lives of orphaned African children adversely affected the lives of children living with their parents. The difficulties which she reveals show the weakness of humanitarian intervention in the absence of access to universal child welfare. Although concerns to promote and safeguard children's well-being are at the centre of child welfare, access to support may be denied in practice. The internet is a valuable resource for exploring reports about the plight of children across the world. The images posted by different charities and children's organisations provide a rich source for students to explore. Students can access and interpret these images and stories of children's lives, which helps them to appreciate the ways in which children's welfare informs children's rights (for an example exercise, please refer to Box 1.3: Media presentations of children in need). Stainton Rogers (2001) describes how child welfare is based on the promotion of the idea that children are entitled to a 'good childhood' and need protection. But perhaps it is also seeing the possibility of a different future which has also assisted in promoting these ideas. It is this which

BOX 1.3: MEDIA PRESENTATIONS OF CHILDREN IN NEED

Choose a children's charity or organisation which you are familiar with and find images about children's lives which are used by charities or organisations to publicise their work.

1. Identify what is being said about the child and their needs from the images you have selected.
2. In your own words describe ***one*** child's needs and identify why they are in need (maximum of 100 words).
3. What does your description show about concerns the charity or organisation has about what is happening to children? Try to identify why children are considered to ***be in need*** and what this means to you.

The aim of the exercise is to review images of children and the ways in which children's needs are presented by children's charities and organisations. We are all familiar with charity appeals to support *children in need*. The images posted by different charities and children's organisations provide a rich source for students to explore.

When children are at the centre of the story, students can scrutinise the messages behind these stories and how the media presents concerns about what is happening to children. By exploring how concerns are presented, and how these frame issues of child welfare and children's rights, students critically evaluate the evidence and begin to see children's rights within a human rights agenda. The same argument applies to child welfare: a child-centred focus is a pre-condition for giving children a voice in what happens to them. Freeman (2009) highlights how it is only when children are seen as individuals, as subject and as persons in their own right, that their rights will be recognised as part of the human rights agenda.

helps to frame the ideals behind interventions which seek to develop the child and those which aim to do this through a children's rights framework.

The twin themes of childhood as a time for enjoyment which emerged in modern society, and a time for happiness, in post-modern society, help to sustain the idea in the West that childhood should be a period of freedom (Stainton Rogers, 2001). The child should be free to grow and develop. They should be liberated from labour, and from adult worries. The child, however, remains the object of child welfare, and in this view of the child as dependent on others, it is possible to trace the legacy of the child saving movement (Therborn, 1996). Children can never be entirely free subjects because of their dependent status (Franklin, 1995, 2002; Freeman, 2009). It may explain why the needs of the child have been framed differently in the phases of development of Unicef. Yet collectively these strategies form the basis of meeting children's well-being. The history of these different approaches provides a salutary lesson of what is possible.

Looking to the future

When we look to the future and imagine a different world we may seek to make a difference to children's lives to improve their welfare (for an example exercise, please refer to Box 1.4: Looking to the future). Reynaert et al. (2009) have interpreted how the quest to improve children's lives begins by focusing on the institutions in which children are educated and cared for, together with recognition of the growing separation of children's lives from adults. The approach encourages scrutiny of practice in order to develop methods of working with children based on critical awareness. Furthermore, Alanen (2011: 147) argues for the need to develop critical awareness to develop disciplinary knowledge:

> Produced by childhood researchers, by way of listening to children and conveying their perspectives into the knowledge of the state of childhood, is meant – and believed – to help in improving the social standing of children and childhood in social life, and to enhance children's well-being in their actual everyday circumstances. In this sense, we might argue that Childhood Studies has the self-understanding of being critical social science, destined to make a difference in the world. Thus, making explicit the normative foundations of childhood research requires that we also address a number of normative issues concerning the practices and arrangements 'out there', and specify in what particular respects and for what specific reasons they are problematic.

The development of the kinds of knowledge described by Alanen (2011) is also related to children's rights. In the West the child has become more visible in the family and as object of social welfare. Increasingly, children's everyday world is the focus of research both in the family and in early years settings (Pahl, 2009; Alanen, 2011; James, 2010). Freeman (2009) explores how children's lives are controlled both to ensure their development and to protect them from harm. However, King (2007) is critical of the social constructivist perspective and questions if it is possible to fully identify with children's agency and apply these to children's rights. Children's agency is bounded by adult intervention, so when adult voices are raised it is their concerns which are prioritised (Franklin, 1995, 2002).

Advocacy

Finding the most effective and efficient way to implement children's rights continues to dominate discussion on children's rights. Reynaert et al. (2009) identify the different elements of what is a technocratic discourse focusing on methods used to monitor rights. Advocacy plays a key role in these strategies together with campaigns which promote change. However, the representation

BOX 1.4: LOOKING TO THE FUTURE – USE OF FACE-TO-FACE AND/OR ONLINE DISCUSSION GROUP

1. Each member of the group must search for one project or campaign which seeks to improve children's lives, in relation to children's participation. Before you begin your search decide which country you will focus on and then select your individual project or campaign. Use the internet to find your example. A useful source is the Unicef site (**www.unicef.org.uk**).
2. Briefly outline in your own words (150 words) the work being done by the project/campaign to support children's participatory rights and share this with the rest of your group. Please remember to identify your source/s of information. If you are using an online discussion area provided by your school/college or university you can post your stories as an attachment to your individual summary. Other members of the group must respond to your posting by adding their own comment on what they see as special to the project/campaign. If you are meeting face to face in class you can share your evidence and put this together to make a poster to show what is special about the project/s.
3. In your group you will identify the strategies being used by the projects/campaigns and show the different ways in which they have supported children's participation. You must identify the factors which contribute to their success and those which act as barriers. If you are using an online discussion area you will need to post your ideas and together produce a written summary (300 words). If you are meeting face to face in class you can discuss you ideas and produce a summary to add to your poster.

From the exercise students recognised the barriers to children's participation (Fortin, 2008). However, students retained a vision about what constituted a better way of life for children and it was this which galvanised their appraisals of the success of individual projects. By focusing on the evidence they had collected, students explored strategies used in practice to promote children's engagement to promote children's welfare.

The exercise helps to transcend philosophical questions about children's rights which appear abstract and to make the link between theory and practice.

of children's lives is problematic because it may heighten children's vulnerability and if so this appeals more to child protectionism than participation.

Monitoring standards

Monitoring progress acts as a catalyst for debate on policy change (Woll, 2000). A key aspect of this is the call for indicators to measure outcomes. Ben-Arieh and George (2001) note that by monitoring children's rights, new domains are explored that go beyond reporting on the survival aspects of children's lives. We promote our ideas of a good childhood and this can create the impression that we measure standards against the norms and expectations of a Western childhood.

Perhaps more than ever with the use of social media, it is the images we select to illustrate children's lives, to show suffering and to present different futures which are powerful.

Summary and conclusion

The influence of the UNCRC, 1989 on setting children's rights as a global human rights issue has been examined (Franklin, 1995, 2002). This chapter explores links between children's rights and child welfare to reveal how concerns about the state of childhood influence action to improve their lives. The history of Unicef and its four phases of development reveal different strategies to address the needs of children (Black, 1996; Knutsson, 1997; Kaufman and Rizzini, 2009). The last phase, which stresses the rights of the child, focuses on provision, protection and participation rights. A more child-centred approach to child welfare is encouraged by children's rights to participation. There are parallels between valuing the contribution of children's participation and seeing children as active social actors, with ethnographic methods used in research with children (Pahl, 2009; Alanen, 2011; James, 2010), some of which are explored in later chapters. The barriers to implementation of children's rights continue to exist, largely because of the tensions between children's rights and parental rights.

Points to consider and questions to ask yourself

- What is special about children's rights compared to rights for adults?
- Identify the barriers to children's participation and consider the different ways you could address these in your practice.
- By showing the relationship between children's rights and child welfare it positions children's participation as critical to creating child-centred services. Consider what lessons can be drawn from research with children and how these can be used to create more child-centred provision.

References

Alanen, L. 2011. Critical Childhood Studies. *Childhood*, 18 (2): 147–150.

Ben-Arieh, A. and George, R. 2001. Beyond the numbers: how do we monitor the state of our children? *Children and Youth Services Review*, 23 (8): 603–631.

Black, M. 1996. *Children First: The Story of UNICEF, Past and Present*. New York: Oxford University Press with United Nations Children's Fund.

Burman, E. 2008. Developing differences: gender, childhood and economic development, in *Developments: Child, Image, Nation*. Hove: Routledge.

Cheney, K. 2010. Expanding vulnerability, dwindling resources: implications for orphaned futures in Uganda. *Childhood in Africa*, 2 (1): 8–15.

CRAE's summary of the Convention on the Rights of the Child. n.d. Article 31. [Online]. Available at http://www.crae.org.uk/rights/uncrc.html. Accessed March 14, 2013.

Davidson, J.O. 2011. Moving children? Child trafficking, child migration and child rights. *Critical Social Policy*, 31: 454–477.

Davies, S. and Artaraz, K. 2009. Towards an understanding of factors influencing early years professionals' practice of consultation with young children. *Children and Society*, 23 (1): 57–69.

DfES (Department of Education and Skills). 2005. Common Core of Skills and Knowledge for the Children's Workforce. Nottingham. Publications [Online] Accessible from www.dcfs.gov.uk/everychildmatters/ strategy/deliveringservices1/commoncore/commoncoreofskillsandknowledge/. Accessed February 20, 2010.

Ennew, J. 2008. Children as 'citizens' of the United Nations (UN), in J. Williams and A. Invernizzi (eds). *Children and Citizenship*. London: Sage.

Fortin, J. 2008. Children as rights holders: awareness and scepticism, in J. Williams and A. Invernizzi (eds). *Children and Citizenship*. London: Sage.

Franklin, B. (ed.) 1995. *The Handbook of Children's Rights: Comparative Policy and Practice.* London: Routledge.

Franklin, B. 2002. Children's rights and media wrongs: changing representations of children and developing rights agenda, in B. Franklin (ed.). *The New Handbook of Children's Rights: Comparative Policy and Practice* (2nd edn). London/New York: Routledge.

Freeman M. 1995. The morality of cultural pluralism. *International Journal of Children's Rights*, 3: 1–17.

Freeman, M. 2000. The future of children's rights. *Children and Society*, 14 (4): 277–293.

Freeman, M. 2009. Children's rights as human rights: reading the UN Convention on the Rights of the Child, in J. Qvortrup, W. Corsaro and M.-S. Honig (eds). *The Palgrave Handbook of Childhood Studies.* Basingstoke: Palgrave.

Gittins, D. 1998. *The Child in Question.* Basingstoke: Macmillan.

Hagglund, S. and Thelander, N. 2011. Children's rights at 21: policy, theory, practice. *Education Inquiry*, 2 (3): 365–372.

Hoffman, D. 2012. Saving children, saving Haiti? Child vulnerability and narratives of nation. *Childhood*, 19 (2): 155–168.

James, A. L. 2010. Competition or integration? The next step in childhood studies? *Childhood*, 17 (4): 485–499.

Johansson, B. 2010. Doing adulthood in childhood research. *Childhood*, 19 (1): 101–114.

Jones, P. 2011. What are children's rights? Contemporary developments and debates, in P. Jones and G.Walker (eds). *Children's Rights in Practice.* London: Sage.

Kaufman, N. H. and Rizzini, I. 2009. Closing the gap between rights and realities of children's lives, in J. Qvortrup, W. Corsaro and M.-S. Honig (eds). *The Palgrave Handbook of Childhood Studies.* Basingstoke: Palgrave.

King, M. 2007. The sociology of childhood as scientific communication: observations from a social systems perspective. *Childhood*, 14 (2): 193–213.

Knutsson, K. E. 1997. *Children: Noble Causes or Worthy Citizens?* New York: Arena/UNICEF.

MacNaughton, G., Hughes, P. and Smith, K. 2007. Young children's rights and public policy: practices and possibilities for citizenship. *Children and Society*, 21: 458–469.

McDowell, J. and Lyons, F. 2009. Improving outcomes for young children: a review of evaluated interventions. *Highlight*, No. 247. London: National Children's Bureau.

Milne, B. 2008. From chattels to citizens? Eighty years of Eglantyne Jebb's legacy to children and beyond, in J. Williams and A. Invernizzi (eds). *Children and Citizenship*. London: Sage.

Pahl, K. 2009. Interactions, intersections and improvisations: studying the multimodal texts and classroom talk of six- to seven-year-olds. *Journal of Early Childhood Literacy*, 9 (2): 188–210.

Papatheodorou, T. and Moyles, J. (eds). 2009. *Learning Together in the Early Years*. Abingdon: Routledge.
Papatheodorou, T. and Moyles, J. 2012. Introduction, in T. Papatheodorou and J. Moyles (eds). *Cross-cultural Perspectives in Early Childhood*. London: Sage.
Penn, H. 2011. Travelling policies and global buzzwords: how international non-governmental organisations and charities spread the word about early childhood in the global South. *Childhood*, 18 (1): 94–113.
Reynaert, D., Bouverne-De Bie, M. and Vandevelde, S. 2009. A review of children's rights literature since the adoption of the United Nations Convention on the Rights of the Child. *Childhood*, 16 (4): 518–534.
Reynolds, P., Nieuwenhuys, O. and Hanson, K. 2006. Refractions of children's rights in development practice: a view from anthropology. *Childhood*, 13 (3): 291–302.
Roche, J. 1999. Children: rights, participation and citizenship. *Childhood*, 6 (4): 475–493.
Stainton Rogers, W. 2001. Constructing childhood: constructing child concern, in P. Foley, J. Roche and S. Tucker (eds). *Children in Society*. Basingstoke: Palgrave/Open University.
Therborn, G. 1996. Child politics, dimensions and perspectives. *Childhood*, 3: 29–44.
Tomas, C. 2008. Childhood and rights: reflections on the UN Convention on the Rights of the Child. *Childhoods Today*, 2 (2): 1–14.
UN Committee on the Rights of the Child. 2005. General Comment No. 7: Implementing Child Rights in Early Childhood. [Online]. Available at http://www2.ohchr.org/english/bodies/crc/docs/AdvanceVersions/GeneralComment7Rev1.pdf. Accessed February 10, 2012.
Wall, J. 2011. Can democracy represent children? Towards a politics of difference. *Childhood*, 19 (1): 86–100.
Woodhead, M. 2008. Promoting young children's development: implications of the UN Convention on the Rights of the Child, in L. Miller and C. Cable (eds). *Professionalism in the Early Years*. London: Hodder Education.
Woll. L, 2000. Organizational responses to the Convention on the Rights of the Child: International lessons for child welfare organizations. *Child Welfare League of America*, 80 (5): 668–679.

Terminology explained

Ethnography: Originating in anthropology, this term traditionally refers to a practice in which researchers spend long periods living within a culture in order to study it. Researchers become part of the everyday life and may observe and/or interact with participants in areas of their lives.

Human capital theory: Providing investment to raise productivity. The theory is also used to promote use of early childhood education and care to support young children's early learning and development. Where these programmes are supported by government funding the aim is to raise the educational achievement of the most disadvantaged children. These programmes are closely monitored to ensure that there is a high rate of return on investment.

Humanitarian intervention: Use of action, including threats, even the use of forces, and sanctions, with the aim of intervening to prevent suffering and harm to children and adults in another country. The intervention is organised and delivered from outside the country where there is suffering.

Institutionalisation of childhood: Describes the use of institutions and institutional care to meet the needs of groups of children to provide for their education and welfare, for example children with disabilities and orphans. The idea of institutionalisation has been used to explain the growing interest in childhood and provision of services for children. Institutions also include early childhood education and care, and institutionalisation, the ways in which these services prepare children for the next stage of their learning.

Modern society: Describes the period in Europe from the late eighteenth century and early nineteenth centuries when industrialisation transformed people's lives. The growth of capitalism created new methods of producing goods and changed people's working lives which affected families and transformed communities. With the introduction of factories many people moved to towns for employment and away from rural areas. Modernity is a term used to explain progress and reflects the idea that our lives will be subject to change. Modern societies are compared with traditional societies which are based on a rural economy and village communities.

Philanthropic action: Money, time and resources are given by individuals to help poor people.

Post-modern society: Describes a post-industrial period associated with the introduction of the information age and knowledge economy. There is no exact date, or agreed period, when European societies ceased to be modern. The term is used to express the way in which use of computers and a networked society has led to changes in the ways we use knowledge to shape our lives.

Protectionism: Advocacy which is used to promote systems and policies to protect children from harm, i.e. child protection. The term is also used in business to describe advocacy, systems, or theory of protecting business from external threats.

CHAPTER

2 Childhood and children's participation

A social-cultural perspective

Mallika Kanyal

Aims of the chapter

1. To give an outline of the history of understanding childhood.
2. To theorise children's participation from a socio-cultural perspective.
3. To emphasise the pedagogical value of adopting a rights-based approach to education.

Introduction

Childhood, as a concept, has been contested for ages and has evolved with the development of academic disciplines and the changing sociological, political and educational landscape. The chapter outlines some of the major changes in our understanding of the term 'childhood', from an academic, rights and pedagogical perspective, by taking examples from an education context. It further theorises participation using a socio-cultural lens of meaning making, which acknowledges the variance and impact of social and cultural practices on children's education. The chapter also shares an example from practice to show how socio-cultural theory can help us deconstruct early childhood pedagogy and understanding of children's participation.

The history of childhood

There have been numerous changes in our understanding of the term 'childhood' and the expectations of children's capabilities and behaviours, which are evident from the study of the history of childhood (Penn, 2005). One of the influential theories of childhood was put forward by Aries and Postman who assert that children were not understood and treated any differently from adults until the sixteenth and seventeenth centuries (cited in Penn, 2005 and Clark, 2010). They were treated with affection, but were generally perceived as underdeveloped adults (Clark, 2010). Aries substantiated his claims by looking at the historical documents and pictorial evidence which included children. His thesis, however, is not untouched from criticism; Tucker (1977), for example, challenges the phallocentric view that Aries presents about children as it lacks the perceptions of children by mothers and nurses.

Postman concurs with Aries' views and further links the invention of childhood with the development of technology, particularly the printing press, around 1459 (Clark, 2010: 18). With the invention of the printing press, books could now be produced with relative ease, opening a world of abstract knowledge and new ideas, gradually separating childhood from adulthood, and making childhood a separate time set apart for learning (Clark, 2010). By the eighteenth century, there emerged a general perception that childhood is a distinct phase of life, recognised differently from adulthood in a number of ways, such as children's separate clothing, games and pastimes, and there was a growing sense of the recognition of innocence of childhood (Lowe, 2004: 66) in the society.

Industrialisation (in the North) in the eighteenth and nineteenth centuries paved the way for the establishment of industrial schools, generally to keep the (poor) children away from the streets. Here (poor) children used to find small, repetitive jobs, such as knitting and nail making; but gradually with the introduction of welfare, education legislation and universal education, more schools were opened, but still remained mainly as educational factories for young children (Penn, 2005). It must not be forgotten that in most societies children were needed as part of the workforce to sustain the economy (and so is the case even now in some societies) and therefore not too many resources were spent on the particular needs of children (Lowe, 2004). The 'modern' sense of childhood appeared with the appearance of a more comfortable 'middle class', who could afford to postpone the entry of their children to the labour market (Lowe, 2004).

Lowe (2004) further points towards underlying issues which emerged with the concept of childhood, two of which are summarised below. He first refers to the two opposing (European) views of childhood, a school of literature which suggests the child is intrinsically evil, right from the time of birth, or at least in need of improvement by adults. Contradictory to the innate evil view was that of children being born as 'innocent' and then being corrupted by the surrounding world. The second underlying issue questions the biological and the social construction of childhood and again throws two differing views of understanding childhood, one that suggests that there are distinct stages of development through which *all* children pass; or childhood is defined by the experiences and treatments which children get from the world where they live and grow.

These popular beliefs and schools of literature gradually paved the way for the development of distinct fields of studying childhood, which have been constantly constructed and reconstructed by theorists and scholars, adding to the richness and scholarship of academic discourses. The discourses have been defined and shaped by the disciplines and regulatory powers that then exhibit control over what could be contemplated about childhood/children by individuals and the profession in general (Cannella, 2005). These dominant discourses therefore seem to control the mainstream of childhood studies, influencing what is studied, researched and generalised under these different disciplines, such as sociology, developmental psychology and anthropology.

The section below outlines the construction of the term 'childhood' as projected by different academic disciplines – namely, sociology, developmental psychology, anthropology and new sociology of childhood – and also as projected by the children's rights movement.

Childhood from a sociological, developmental psychology and social-cultural perspective

As seen from the history of childhood, children were generally seen as passive beings, as incompetent organisms; and childhood was seen as a period for preparation for adulthood. In the early twentieth century, the field of sociology developed, which studied human relationships in society(ies), but with very little explicit mention of childhood (Thomas, 2004). Childhood was mainly referenced in sociology through 'family', 'education' or through the process of 'socialisation'. Socialisation, as a process, again reinstated the common belief that children are the prospective members of a society as opposed to actual and participating (Thomas, 2004). The same belief propagated in the 1960s (Gabriel, 2007), through yet another academic discipline, called child rearing psychology, which then became the dominant field in education. It studied and looked for ways of turning the immature, irrational and incompetent child into a mature, rational and competent adult (Gabriel, 2007: 80). These dominant principles were at the heart of developmental psychology, where children were valued more for their future as adults than for their present lives as children (Gabriel, 2007: 80).

Developmental psychology, as a branch of psychology, has offered rich insight into children's learning and development, but mainly from a Euro-American perspective. When compared with the field of sociology, it is convergent with the interactionist perspective, which emerged as a strong critique of socialisation theory, and laid the foundation for studying adult–child and child–child interaction, for understanding the complexity of human group life (Thomas, 2004). Developmental psychology, therefore, can be said to have filled some of the gaps in sociological theories as it started looking at the active role that children play in their learning, a concept very different from socialisation theory. Developmental psychology uses key concepts such as **learning**, **conditioning** and **unfolding**, described in various child psychology theories, such as the ones put forward by Jean Piaget, Margaret Donaldson and Lev Vygotsky. These concepts and theories tell us about children's active participation in learning; the appropriateness of the learning environment and the importance of dialogue and negotiation in cultural learning (Thomas, 2004). The value and contribution of developmental psychology in the construction of childhood, therefore, cannot be underestimated, but at the same time it gave rise to universal averages and education models (such as Developmentally Appropriate Practice – DAP), the principles of which were recognised as a norm and its milestones as targets for all children across the continents, regardless of their local needs, priorities and contexts. Developmental psychology became the dominant discourse in understanding children's education for many decades in the twentieth century and therefore propagated the Western construction of childhood across the globe (Dahlberg et al., 1999). It contributed to a system where children were seen simultaneously by what they can do and what they cannot; by their deficit; by their next step; by the developmental milestone that they are yet to achieve.

Prout and James (1990) argued for the further development of different versions of childhood, critiquing on the universal and standard models, based primarily on the experiences of children in rich countries. They argued for the acceptance of social construction of childhood, based on the belief that young children get socialised in different ways, depending upon where they live and grow. This framework enabled a comparative and cultural analysis to identifying different childhoods in diverse contexts (Gabriel, 2007). Yelland and Kilderry (2005) similarly urge us to move away from a binary understanding of childhood experiences (*developmentally appropriate* against *inappropriate* and *normal* against *abnormal*) and consider new frameworks to capture the complexity of lifeworlds experienced by our children today.

With the emerging critique of developmental psychology, it was soon realised that social structures play a vital role in children's learning and development, theorised academically by various psychologists such as Urie Bronfenbrenner and Lev Vygotsky, under the banner of socio-cultural approach, especially in the 1980s. Bronfenbrenner (1979), through his ecological framework, explains how an interaction between the micro-systems (family), meso-systems (pre-school and school), macro-systems (economic and social policies) of cultures and societies and chrono-systems (time) influence conditions for children's learning and development. Similarly, Vygotsky's (1986) socio-cultural theory suggests that children's social and cultural knowledge evolves as children actively engage with their environments. When applying these principles to pedagogic practice, these theories define a teacher's role to encourage and allow children to participate in collaborative tools with (more competent) peers and adults around them and propagated a belief that learning and teaching is context bound (Jamieson et al., 2000).

Taking the theoretical argument further, educator Barbara Rogoff, with her work on different cultures, further bridges psychology with anthropology, and drawing on Vygotsky's work she introduces a cultural-historical perspective of human development. Rogoff makes reference to Vygotsky's and Dewey's theories focusing on children's participation in socio-cultural activities, with other people, in a seamless order (Rogoff, 1995). When applied to education, children are seen to be learning by interacting with other members of the society who are more conversant with the society's practices and tools for mediating intellectual activity (Vygotsky, 1978 and 1987, in Rogoff, 1995).

Rogoff (2007) suggests that individuals develop as participants in their cultural communities where they *engage* and work *with* each other and hence build on cultural practices of previous generations. She therefore refers to childhood and childhood construction(s) from a *cultural-historical* perspective where an individual's perceptions, community as well as cultural-historical traditions and materials play an important role in shaping childhood experiences. She, however, cautions against labelling people according to their cultures, as culture, contrary to its common perception of being static, is a dynamic and ever changing phenomenon which alters with time through generations' work (Olusoga, 2009). Schneider and Evans (2008) echo Rogoff's ideas into education, agreeing that it is the 'interdependence of individual mind, interpersonal relations and social situations that enable learning or development'. To enable the learning process, children therefore need to possess a sense of belonging to the community, identify themselves as members, and share common values for learning processes (Schneider and Evans, 2008).

Childhood from a new sociology of childhood and children's rights perspective

The above discussion implies that children's learning and development is hugely influenced by the social structures, culture, guidance and support they receive from adults, which may vary depending upon the place where they live and grow. It is this variance that recognises the multiplicity in childhood(s) and enriches our understanding of the 'social construction of childhood'. Childhood, therefore, is socially constructed and each society creates its own concept of what childhood means (Sleep, 2010). The attempt made by the United Nations Convention on the Rights of the Children (United Nations, 1989), however, can be seen to be unifying childhood(s) amongst these differences, especially from a political view. They see *all* children, regardless of where they live, from a framework of 'rights' informed by the human activist approach of 'empowering the disempowered'. Their aim is to protect as well as empower children and provide appropriate services for their well-being. The ratification of the UNCRC (post 1989) by state parties therefore gave children a political status, recognising them as rights bearers, articulated clearly in the 54 articles of the UNCRC.

The ideals of childhood as upheld by the UNCRC closely resonate with the ideals of the academic discipline of 'new sociology of childhood'. They both reposition the traditional view of children being 'passive' with that of being 'active' members in the society, a concept which values children's agency as participants within their communities. Recognition of children's agency is expressed explicitly through Article 12 of the UNCRC, which states:

> 1. Parties shall assure to the child, who is capable of forming his or her own views, the right to express those views freely in all matters affecting the child, the views of the child being given due weight in accordance with the age and maturity of the child.
>
> 2. For this purpose the child shall in particular be provided the opportunity to be heard in any judicial and administrative proceedings affecting the child, either directly, or through a representative or an appropriate body, in a manner consistent with the procedural rules of national law.
>
> (UN Committee on the Rights of the Child, 2009: 3)

Educationists and sociologists like Alan Prout, Allison James and William Corsaro have made distinctive contributions to advancing this new area of study. They identify some distinctive features of the new sociology of childhood, such as childhood is a social construction; it is a variable of social analysis which intersects with other social variables, such as class, gender, ethnicity; children's relationships are worthy of studying in their own right; children must be seen as actively contributing and determining their own social lives (Prout and James, in Thomas, 2004); and that children actively contribute to cultural production and change, are constrained by the existing social structures, but within these constraints, their participation is creative and innovative (Corsaro, in Thomas, 2004: 81). These features make the new sociology of childhood distinct from other areas of sociology as it gives children a distinct voice and participation in the production of sociological data (Prout and James, 1990).

The methods of study used in the new sociology of childhood and children's rights approach therefore give a definitive status to children's voice and their participation. The new sociology of childhood includes children's perspectives and their participation in various social, educational and judiciary processes, making use of (child-centred) participatory methods (Lundy and McEvoy, 2012). The rights approach takes the adult–child relationship a little further and makes it an obligatory one where adults *have* to respect children's entitlement to express their views about their own lives, and more importantly, also help *form* them (Lundy and McEvoy, 2012). Children's rights, therefore, could be argued to be seeing children's participation from a 'capacity building' perspective, synonymous with Lensmire's (1998), Maybin's (2001) and Wyness's (2006) suggestion that children's voice (and therefore their participation) needs to be regarded as a 'project', a 'struggle' and a 'friendly space' (cited in Kellett, 2010), and in order to enable participation, adults need to provide them with a discursive space to be able to experiment and develop their voices (Lundy, 2007).

Children's participation and the cultural-historical perspective

Moving on from childhood to children's participation and the idea of a discursive space, these can be explained using Rogoff's ideas of 'apprenticeship', 'guided participation' and 'participatory appropriation' (Rogoff, 1995), all essential aspects of the cultural-historical perspective of human development, illustrated in Figure 2.1. Rogoff regards the three elements as inseparable as they reflect the three foci in socio-cultural activities – community/institutional; interpersonal; and personal.

- The metaphor of **apprenticeship** links with the plane of community. Here individuals participate with each other in culturally organised activities and help the less experienced seek maturity, for example schooling.
- The concept of **guided participation** operates at an interpersonal plane and refers to various processes and systems of involvement that are used to communicate and coordinate with each other, including both face-to-face as well as distal activities. 'Participation' within 'guided participation' refers to both observations as well as hands-on involvement in activities, and 'guided' refers to the direction offered by social partners, culture and social values.

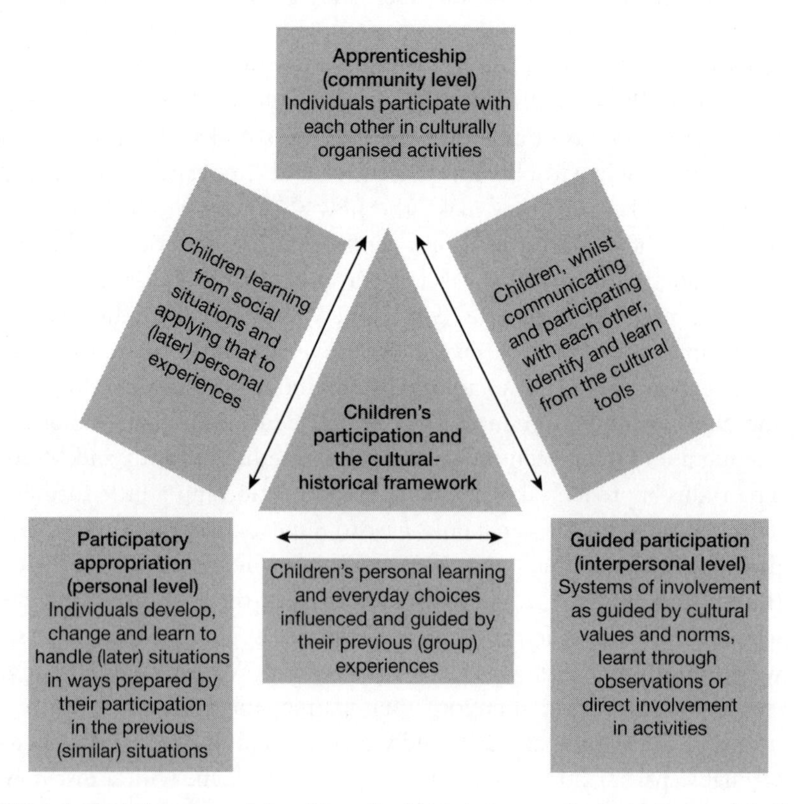

FIGURE 2.1 An illustrative representation of the cultural-historical perspective to children's participation

In other words, it refers to the choices we make in our everyday lives – shaped and guided by our social experiences, cultural values and traditions.

- **Participatory appropriation** operates at a 'personal' level where individuals change and develop through their involvement and engagement in activities. These engagements are guided by the cultural-historic frameworks. Individuals learn to handle situations by learning from their previous experiences and participation. Rogoff argues 'participatory appropriation' to be a process of 'becoming' rather than 'acquisition' as in the other two.

As apparent from the above discussion, it is vital to provide opportunities for children to engage in various social and cultural activities, under the guidance of others (adults). At the same time, it is important to provide them with a discursive space where they can experiment and test their ideas. It is this combination of guided participation and the discursive space which enables children to form informed views about their own learning and learning environments. An example below (Box 2.1), a case study, described by Michelle Barker, an Early Years Professional (EYP) at the Saplings Nursery in Henham (Bishop's Stortford), Hertfordshire, shows how children are encouraged to participate within their (learning) environments. Children, through their participation, form tools of engagement that have the potential to take their (and adults') learning forward. 'Saplings' is a private day nursery for children aged 3 months to 5 years, and has been operating since December 1998. They are located in a rural setting with a large outside area for the children to access. The example below makes use of this outside space to allow children to experiment with their ideas and form a participative space which offers potential for both pedagogy and play.

The project shown in Box 2.1 clearly demonstrates how children are provided with the local tools and affordances to create a shared environment where they can participate in various individual as well as group activities (Rogoff's community/institutional lens). The help and support from adults (practitioners and parents) emphasise the 'guided' nature of participation, guidance in the form of adults' help in both collecting and putting the tools together as well as passing on the value of recycling and working together, which is anticipated to help children learn and develop. The concept of 'participatory appropriation' can also be applied here as children's participation in this and other similar activities within the nursery will act as a progressive learning tool for children which can potentially develop and change the ways they interact and engage within their learning environments. An appropriate provision of a discursive space (both physical and mental), where children can experiment and test their ideas, is therefore essential to put a participative paradigm into practice. The ways of doing this could be different in different social-cultural contexts which are further inspired by the local traditions, beliefs and availability of resources.

The example cited above is also in direct contrast with the traditional and didactic teacher-centred pedagogy which only asserts teachers' authority over learning and teaching processes (Papatheodorou, 2010). It advocates Article 12

BOX 2.1: CASE STUDY, SAPLINGS NURSERY, HENHAM, HERTFORDSHIRE

In accordance with the EYFS, particularly the principle of 'Enabling environments', which states that the outdoor environment has a positive impact on all areas of a child's development by offering them firsthand experiences, it is our duty, as early years practitioners, to ensure that the children at our settings have access to a good quality outdoor learning environment. The outdoors is a rich and dynamic space for high quality learning to take place which the children enjoy.

Having qualified from Anglia Ruskin University with a BA in Early Years and Education and an Early Years Professional status, I was keen to put into practice some positive changes. With all staff on board and the garden as our focus for this term, we wanted to create a varied and diverse environment with meaningful and engaging experiences. For some children spending a lot of time at Saplings and it being like a second home, we wanted the children to help organise their own environment and be part of the creation. Allowing the children to have a voice, express their opinions and make decisions focuses on Article 12 of the UNCRC, which suggests that children should have the right to say what they think and have their ideas taken into account, especially if the decision being made by an adult affects the children directly.

The first stage of the project took place at the start of the summer term 2012. The initial idea was to have a group discussion with the pre-school children aged 40–50 months, who primarily use the front garden area for outdoor play. Within small groups to support children's confidence, we had discussions about the garden area and what the children currently like doing outside. A plan was created out of the children's initial ideas (see Figure 2.2).

At a later stage we invited the children to express their ideas through illustrations (for examples, see children's drawings, Figure 2.3) where the children had individual time-out to show their opinions of the outdoor environment. At the third stage children were interviewed separately and were asked 1) What they like doing in the setting garden, 2) What they like doing in their gardens at home, 3) Where they like going outside of nursery, like the forest or park, and 4) What they would like to have in the garden at nursery. At a final stage the children had opportunities to capture their favourite areas in the setting outside, using a camera.

One challenge that occurred was to ensure that all children had the chance to express their opinions including our children with additional needs or English as an additional language. To ensure these children were given the chance to express ideas, we created a visual board of pictures from our outdoor areas and other environments or activities for the children to visually make a choice from and stick onto a map of our garden area. We also joined in partnership with our parents, asking them to voice record phrases or words expressed by the child about the garden area, using a voice recording phonic book in their home language. With contact from our area Ethnic Minority Support Officer we

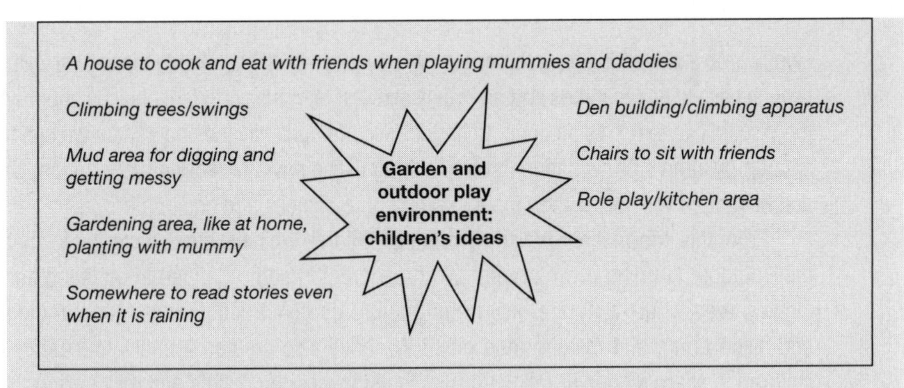

FIGURE 2.2 A plan created out of children's ideas on the use of outdoor space

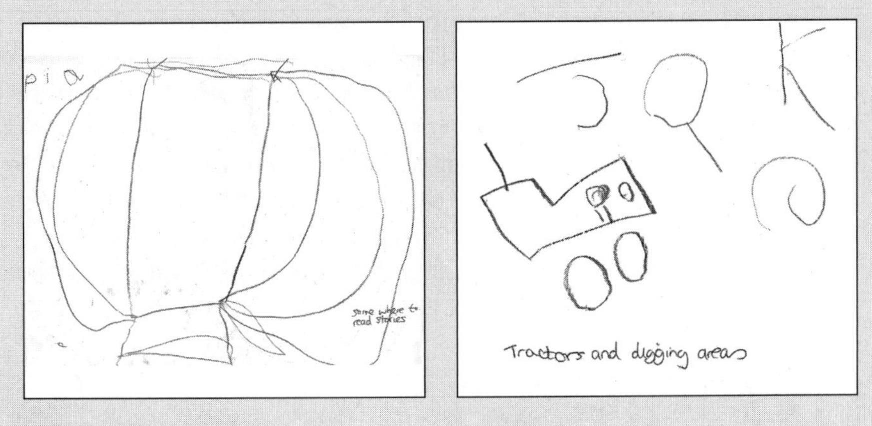

FIGURE 2.3 Somewhere to read stories and . . . tractor and digging area

were also able to loan equipment such as the 'penpal' resource which allows you to record or scan words and phrases in different languages in order to support children's voice, whichever language they speak first.

At a staff meeting, the pre-school team helped me analyse the findings from the children's group discussion, individual interviews and the children's illustrations. The findings suggest that children wanted the following from their outdoor space:

(i) to have areas to go with their friends to spend time either reading stories, or talking with each other,
(ii) to do digging in mud patches,
(iii) to have an outdoor cooking area.

As a follow up, I organised our staff training event around 'Communication Friendly Spaces' and we audited our environment looking at whether there are enough defined areas for children to spend time free playing and talking with peers. We also did some practical tasks with staff gathering resources for the children to use and allowing them to create their own spaces and learning environment in the way they would like. Within the setting children have access to all resources and are freely allowed to make confident choices about what they would like to do. As an ongoing project, we are currently looking at how we can fully support children's participation in the planning of the environment on a permanent basis and how often we review their input into resource choices and equipment.

From this information gathering from our children we have already started to change their outdoor learning environment. We have created some defined areas such as the digging area where they are having fun setting up construction sites, general digging and discovering, and making mud pies!! We have also created friendly spaces for the children to share stories or talk with friends using wooden pallets and milk cartons, and have created seats from tree stumps and logs. Our monthly newsletter is asking parents to support us in creating our outdoor kitchen with items from home such as kitchen units, cookers and microwaves that they might be changing or clearing out. The children can bring in items they have chosen with their parents from home. The children have been involved in collecting the milk cartons from home to make their 'talking space' (see pictures below), and they have been involved in where they would like things to be placed like frames for den building, the vegetable boxes for growing, and logs for seating areas. The children have also been given the chance to help the staff risk assess the environment and have created a 'safety rule board'.

For this project I have taken inspiration from Hart's (1997) ladder of participation, where one of its rungs states that adults can have an initial idea to develop with

children's help. Here, we initiated the garden project as adults, but by allowing our children to be involved in terms of planning, ideas, and decision making, we provided them with a participative space. The garden project at the setting is a huge task and will be on-going for all involved. The staff have started to monitor the children's use of the new areas and resources, and have received very positive feedback from the children who are engaging and enjoying the changes. This use of involving children will continue throughout the nursery environment to revise and change aspects with the children's involvement.

of the UNCRC (UN Committee on the Rights of the Child, 2009) as it shows the belief of the practitioners that a child has a 'capacity to form her or his own views and recognise that she or he has the right to express them' (page 6); 'recognition of, and respect for, non-verbal forms of communication including play, body language, facial expressions, and drawing and painting' (page 7); a determination to ensure that 'children experiencing difficulties in making their views heard', for instance, children with English as an additional language and special education needs, are 'equipped with, and enabled to use, other modes of communication to facilitate the expression of their views' (page 7). The setting, thereby, can be seen as making an effort in providing the children 'with an environment in which they feel respected and secure to freely express their opinions' (page 7).

Pedagogical environments, therefore, when viewed from a rights and social-cultural perspective, offer a 'pedagogy that facilitates and mediates individual and shared activity, forges interaction and interrelationships, generates ideas and action, encourages communication and co-operation and supports independence and interdependence' (Papatheodorou, 2010: 158). It is important for such environments to focus on children 'becoming', but not at the expense of their 'being', 'well-being' and 'belonging' (Papatheodorou, 2010).

Theorising participation

The example from Saplings Nursery shows that children's participation, like childhood, can be seen to be embedded within the theoretical framework of a social-cultural approach, where meaning making is influenced by the social structures and processes, whilst acknowledging the influence of culture and tradition at the same time (Wimpenny, 2010). Children's voice, therefore, needs to be considered with a caveat of not being a linear and individualised voice but an interactional and socially constructed voice (Spyrou, 2011), which can be hugely influenced by the socio-political structures of which children are a part, for example the social class, family background, setting's/school's general environment and their policies.

The pedagogical implication of this paradigm can be summarised through Vygotsky's (1986) socio-cultural theory which suggests that children's social and cultural knowledge evolves as children actively engage with their environments. Children's overall learning, therefore, will be influenced by not only the active learning opportunities but also the hidden curriculum in how they interact with the environment (other children and adults) and objects in the environment (the physical space and resources) within the classroom. The pedagogical quality and processes therefore take shape and develop through the interaction between people, and people and objects, in the learning contexts of institutions. This perspective takes into account the norms, values, traditions, cultural specifics, contextual specifics and heritage of society (Sheridan, 2007). Education settings (schools and early years settings) may be quite different in the ways they perceive education, and hence will vary in how they implement pedagogical processes that support the right of the child to learn and develop, to participate and influence the ongoing processes and activities (Kanyal and Cooper, 2010).

The role of the teacher/practitioner, according to this theory, is therefore to affirm these ideas by allowing children to participate in collaborative tools with (more competent) peers and adults around them, whilst interacting with the physical space. When applying this to young children, these tools can be developed by providing children with the opportunities for free play, for the freedom of expression (Bae, 2009), where both the practitioner and children take part as active participants, sharing knowledge and playfulness.

Children, however, unlike adults, have a hundred languages to express their views (Edwards et al., 2012), a phenomenon which cautions adults to be creative in selecting the most appropriate methods of understanding children's perceptions of the world around them. If these methods are used effectively, they offer not only the opportunity for children to participate in their education, but also the potential to empower them and hone their participatory skills, which can only be a useful thing.

Summary and conclusion

The chapter gives a brief account of the concept of childhood from different theoretical and academic discipline perspectives. It shows the evolving and hence the socially constructed nature of childhood which may vary depending upon the place where children live and grow. Example from practice shows the socially constructed nature of childhood and children's participation where adults provide guidance and opportunities for children to express their views freely and also to test their ideas in a secure and respectful space. These methods of involvement may vary among different cultures where adults draw upon their personal, interpersonal and community experiences to provide appropriately for children's participation.

Points to consider and questions to ask yourself

- How can we provide children with a discursive space to experiment with their views and develop and form a 'voice'? Give some examples.
- How can children be helped to express their (multiple) voices? What methods can be used?
- How do you think your social and cultural knowledge and heritage shapes the experiences that you offer to children? How does it help them form a 'view'?
- How can we offer 'apprenticeship' and 'guided participation' opportunities to young children in care? Make a list. Are these mostly interactional activities or distal (observational) activities? What difference does it make in their experience?

References

Bae, B. 2009. Children's right to participate – challenges in everyday interactions. *European Early Childhood Education Research Journal*, 17 (3): 391–406.

Bronfenbrenner, U. 1979. *The Ecology of Human Development: Experiments by Nature and Design*. London: Harvard University.

Cannella, G. S. 2005. Reconceptualising the field (of early care and education): if western child development is a problem, then what do we do? in N. Yelland (eds). *Critical Issues in Early Childhood Education*. Maidenhead: Open University Press.

Clark, R. M. 2010. *Childhood in Society*. Exeter: Learning Matters.

Dahlberg, G., Moss P. and Pence, A. 1999. *Beyond Quality in Early Childhood Education and Care: Postmodern Perspectives* (1st edn). London: Falmer Press.

Edwards, C., Gandini, L. and Forman, G. (eds). 2012. *The Hundred Languages of Children: The Reggio Experience in Transformation* (3rd edn). Santa Barbara, CA: Praeger.

Gabriel, N. 2007. Children and childhoods, in J. Willan, R. Parker-Rees and J. Savage (eds). *Early Childhood Studies* (2nd edn). Exeter: Learning Matters.

Hart, R. A. 1997. *Children's Participation: The Theory and Practice of Involving Young Citizens in Community Development and Environmental Care*. London: Earthscan.

Jamieson, P., Fisher, K., Gilding, T., Taylor, P. G. and Trevitt, A. D. 2000. Place and space in the design of new environments. *Higher Education Research and Development*, 19: 221–237.

Kanyal, M. and Cooper, L. 2010. Young children's perceptions of their school experience: a comparative study between England and India. *Procedia – Social and Behavioural Sciences*, 2 (2): 3605–3613.

Kellett, M. 2010. Small shoes, big steps! Empowering children as active researchers. *American Journal of Community Psychology*, 46: 195–203.

Lowe, R. 2004. Childhood through ages, in T. Maynard and N. Thomas (eds). *Early Childhood Studies*. London: Sage.

Lundy, L. 2007. 'Voice' is not enough: conceptualising Article 12 of the United Nations Convention on the Rights of the Child. *British Educational Research Journal*, 33 (6): 927–942.

Lundy, L. and McEvoy, L. 2012. Children's rights and research processes: assisting children to (in)formed views. *Childhood*, 19 (1): 129–144.

Olusoga, Y. 2009. We don't play like that here: social, cultural and gender perspectives on play, in A. Brock, S. Dodds, P. Jarvis and Y. Olusoga (eds). *Perspectives on Play*. London: Pearson.
Papatheodorou, T. 2010. The pedagogy of playful learning environments, in J. Moyles (ed.). *Thinking about Play: Developing a Reflective Approach*. Maidenhead: Open University Press.
Penn, H. 2005. Past, present and future, in *Understanding Early Childhood: Issues and Controversies*. Maidenhead: Open University Press.
Prout, A. and James, A. 1990. A new paradigm for the sociology of childhood? Provenance, promise and problems, in A. James and A. Prout (eds). *Constructing and Reconstructing Childhood: Contemporary Issues in the Sociological Study of Childhood*. London: Falmer Press.
Rogoff, B. 1995. Observing sociocultural activity on three planes: participatory appropriation, guided participation, and apprenticeship, in J. V. Wertsch, P. del Rio and A. Alvarez (eds). *Sociocultural Studies of Mind*. Cambridge: Cambridge University Press. Reprinted, 2008, in K. Hall and P. Murphy (eds). *Pedagogy and Practice: Culture and Identities*. London: Sage.
Rogoff, B. 2007. The cultural nature of human development. *The General Psychologist*, 42: 1.
Schneider, S. and Evans, M. 2008. Transforming e-learning into ee-learning: the centrality of sociocultural participation. *Innovate*, 5 (1).
Sheridan, S. 2007. Dimensions of pedagogical quality in pre-school. *International Journal of Early Years Education*, 15 (2): 197–217.
Sleep, K. 2010. A critical examination of how adults' concepts of childhood have informed the proposed recommendations of the Cambridge Primary Review. *The Plymouth Student Educator*, 2 (1): 57–66.
Spyrou, S. 2011. The limits of children's voices: from authenticity to critical, reflexive representation. *Childhood*, 18 (2): 151–165.
Thomas, N. 2004. Sociology of childhood, in T. Maynard and N. Thomas (eds). *An Introduction to Early Childhood Studies*. London: Sage.
Tucker, N. 1977. *What Is a Child?* London: Fontana.
United Nations. 1989. United Nations Convention on the Rights of the Child. [Online]. Available at http://www2.ohchr.org/english/law/crc.htm. Accessed January 13, 2013.
UN Committee on the Rights of the Child. 2009. General Comment No. 12: The right of the child to be heard, 20 July 2009, CRC/C/GC/12. [Online]. Available at http://www.unhcr.org/refworld/docid/4ae562c52.html. Accessed January 15, 2013.
Vygotsky, L. S. 1986. *Thought and Language*. Cambridge, MA: MIT Press.
Wimpenny, K. 2010. Participatory action research: an integrated approach towards practice development, in M. Savin-Baden and C. H. Major (eds). *New Approaches to Qualitative Research: Wisdom and Uncertainty*. London: Routledge.
Yelland, N. and Kilderry, A. 2005. Against the tide: new ways in early childhood education, in N. Yelland (ed.). *Critical Issues in Early Childhood Education*. Maidenhead: Open University Press.

Terminology explained

Anthropology: The science of humanity. It studies the origins, physical and cultural development, biological characteristics and beliefs of humankind. It is derived from the Greek words, *anthropos*, meaning 'man/mankind', and *logia*, meaning 'study'.

Developmentally Appropriate Practice (DAP): Developmentally Appropriate Practice, often referred to as DAP, is regarded as an approach towards teaching and learning, the principles of which are derived from developmental psychology. DAP, usually followed as a pedagogical framework in rich countries, guides teachers to focus on children's (individual as well as group) pre-established targets for learning and development, based on their age and stage of development.

Developmental psychology: A branch of psychology that studies the growth of human beings and the changes that occur in infancy, childhood and throughout the life-span.

Hundred languages: A phrase inspired by Loris Malaguzzi's (founder of the Reggio Emilia approach to early education in Italy) famous poem 'The hundred languages of children'. It means that children can depict their thinking in numerous ways, such as through spoken words as well as other symbolic language like drawings, sculpture, dramatic play, writing, etc.

Interactionist perspective: One of the major theoretical perspectives in sociology which focuses on social processes of human action in everyday life, for example identity, cooperation and conflict; in other words, how individuals act within a society.

Jean Piaget, **Margaret Donaldson** and **Lev Vygotsky**: A group of psychologists, who, through their theories/studies, critiqued the behaviourist approach towards understanding of 'learning'; and instead developed a theoretical kinship by developing the constructivist/social constructivist/socio-cultural constructivist approach towards children's cognitive development. Jean Piaget's name is associated with the 'staged theory' of children's cognitive development which he developed based on his experiments and studies done on children in a laboratory environment. Margaret Donaldson critiqued Piaget's work as underestimating children's cognitive abilities due to the lack of consideration of child friendly environment in his experiments. Lev Vygotsky extended Piaget's work and emphasised the socio-cultural nature of learning, making a significant contribution to our understanding of the role of language and culture in cognitive development.

New sociology of childhood: A paradigm of knowledge which emerged (and is still emerging) as a critique of the sociological tradition of understanding childhood. It challenges the adult-centric view of sociology towards children and emphasises the active role that children play in creating their own childhood culture(s).

Socialisation: A term generally used by sociologists which refers to the process of acquiring social and cultural norms of the society where we live and grow.

Sociology: The study of human society. It explores the origin, development, organisation and functioning of human society.

PART

Children's participation

Theory and practice

CHAPTER

3 Participation

Why and how?

Mallika Kanyal and Jane Gibbs

Aims of the chapter

1. To put forward a case for children's participation by considering arguments 'against' and 'in favour of' participation.
2. To explore barriers to participation from a practitioner's perspective.
3. To understand behavioural issues from a child's perspective and consider providing opportunities for empowerment via a 'Spiral of Empowerment'.

Introduction

In this chapter we discuss how participation has been recognised as an essential entitlement for children, especially in an education and care context. Links are made with international and national initiatives to protect children's participatory rights, with a focus on the challenges faced by the practitioners/teachers in drawing implications of these policies into everyday practice. Emphasis is placed on the opportunities for staff development and training, not necessarily from a top down perspective, but originating from the needs and reflections from a setting, where capacity to promote participation can get built within the critical discussions at staff meetings. How and when children participate depends mainly on the attitudes and behaviours emanated from adults. An addition of in-house training to this chapter, therefore, provides an example in understanding the 'why' and 'how' of participation. A need for encouraging empowerment in children is also recognised and explained through a 'Spiral of Empowerment'.

There have been various movements on children's rights and their participation in history: for example, the Swedish social reformer Ellen Key published *The Century of the Child* in 1909; English social activist Eglantyne Jebb set up the first overseas relief agency – Save the Children Fund – in 1919; Janusz Korczak, a Polish doctor, pedagogue and children's writer, set up an orphanage in Poland and insisted on accompanying the children in his care to their deaths in the Treblinka extermination camp during the Second World War in 1942 (Woodhead, 2010, cited in Percy-Smith and Thomas, 2010); but an unprecedented stimulus has been realised in children's participation with the ratification of the United Nations Convention on the Rights of the Child (UNCRC, 1989) by almost every government in the world (with the exception of Somalia and the United States of America). The Convention has made children's right to participation explicit through its articles, especially through Article 12 (the right of children to participate in decisions affecting them), Article 13 (the right to freedom of expression) and Article 14 (the right to freedom of thought, conscience and religion).

These rights are recently being realised and applied into education contexts through various forms and processes which are believed to offer long-term opportunities for sustained educational experiences (Pascal and Bertram, 2009). Research around children's participation and the changing ideas of childhood also support the notion of children as competent social actors and not as subjects or objects of research. Various research studies have demonstrated the capability and capacity of children to participate in decision making, including their effective contributions in shaping their own learning environments and designing and leading their own research agendas (see Clark and Moss, 2006; Clark, 2010; and Kellett, 2010). The application of these ideas is complex and needs to be understood critically. There are various challenges and scepticism associated with children's meaningful participation, especially in the early years sector. This scepticism, to some extent, has been overcome by the publication of the General Comment No. 7 by the UN Committee on the Rights of the Child (2005). The comment clearly outlines the implementation of child rights in early childhood, a period defined by the UN committee from birth throughout infancy, the pre-school years as well as the transition time to school (UN Committee on the Rights of the Child, 2005).

Within England, a significant interest and commitment to listening to young children has developed since 2000 (Hamer, 2009), evident from recent policy developments, such as the Children Act 2004 and the Childcare Act 2006. The Children Act 2004, for the first time, created the post of Children's Commissioner for England who has the function of promoting awareness of the views and interests of children in England (Children Act 2004). It also places a duty on local authorities to appoint a director of children's services and an elected lead member for children's services, who is ultimately accountable for the delivery of services (NSPCC factsheet, n.d.). The coalition government published revised statutory guidance relating to the two posts in April 2012 (NSPCC factsheet, n.d.). The Childcare Act 2006, section 3.5, also makes a legal requirement on local authorities to listen to young children and states that they must have regard to any information about the views of young children which is available and relevant to childcare duties (Participation Works, n.d.). Early childhood services, therefore, have a crucial role to play in developing a listening culture which nurtures day-to-day listening and provides opportunities for young children to make decisions about matters that directly affect them (Participation Works, n.d.).

The emergence of children's participation has also been evidenced in curriculum development through the introduction of Citizenship classes in secondary schools since 2002; the introduction of the statutory cross-curricular theme of Personal, Social and Health Education in primary schools (Andrews and Mycock, 2007); the beginning of Development Matters, recognised through providing an 'enabling environment' within the Early Years Foundation Stage (EYFS) curriculum (DfE, 2012); a section of the Special Educational Needs Code of Practice (DfES, 2001), along with various other education policies. However, when looking closely at the statutory curriculum frameworks, children's rights are barely mentioned in the (revised) EYFS (DfE, 2012). They are mentioned briefly in the non-statutory guidance materials and not in the statutory framework. Much of the EYFS advises that every child is unique and the practice should support them to be resilient, capable, confident and self-assured; but it seems to stop at this point and does not include any further advice, for example on how this competent child can help to influence practice.

The policies and initiatives, as outlined above, demonstrate a positive step towards promoting children's participatory rights, but there is still scepticism in implementing these ideals into practice. Main concerns have been around the conflict between children's and adults' rights (for details please refer to Chapter 1); multiple interpretations of participation; and an unquestionable acceptance of the traditional paternal approach of adults towards children. A lack of information on how to translate these policies into practice may further dictate application at a tokenistic level. Besides all the uncertainties, the proponents of children's participation have been advocating for the benefits of involving children in a range of social and educational phenomena, not only from a '*becoming*' *(future)*, but also from a '*being*' *(present)*, 'well-being' and 'belonging' perspective (Papatheodorou, 2010). They see children's participation from a value ridden perspective, which acknowledges the gains children make in terms of knowledge, skills, development and empowerment.

Existing tensions in children's participation

Researchers over the past two decades (and earlier) have been propagating for the benefits of children's participation, but a lot of tension still exists when it comes to implementing children's participation in practice. The figure below (Figure 3.1) provides a generic understanding of these tensions.

The figure demonstrates the challenges of applying participatory ideas into practice. It especially points towards the argument around universalisation of the concept of participation through the Convention on the Rights of the Child. The argument can be traced back to the philosophical level as to how we view childhood and its plurality of interpretations when applied in different cultural and/or social contexts. We are very much focusing participation in this chapter around an education context, with a caveat, that what is meaningful in one

Arguments used in favour of participation	Arguments used against participation
Basic human right	Confidentiality issues
Hear issues from children's perspective	Children first in need of skills training
Raises children's self-esteem	Danger of short-term participation
Learn cooperation and important communication skills	Issues regarding informed consent
Initiatives more responsive to the needs of children	May cause emotional harm
Raises public awareness of the needs of children and young people	Children lacking the competence or experience to participate
Minimises the chances of adults abusing their power on children	Issues of rights vs responsibility
Parallels drawn with parents' rights	Burden of responsibility can take away their childhood
Recognition of children's interests, which are often disregarded in public policy	May lead to lack of respect for parents/adults
	Issues of culture
	Protection risks

FIGURE 3.1 Arguments 'in favour of' and 'against' participation

Adapted from Lansdown, G. 2001. *Promoting Children's Participation in Democratic Decision Making.* Florence, Italy: United Nations International Innocenti Research Centre.

context might not be applicable to another. The concept of rights, and consequently children's participation, is therefore affected by the wider social norms to which children belong. Some communities might be quite ahead in accommodating and encouraging children's participation in education whereas others might not be able to treat them as a priority. Their priorities might lie somewhere else, for example in protecting the survival rights of children. The role of adults, therefore, is crucial here, which can be explained using Rogoff's concept of 'guided participation'. She refers to children being actively involved in their communities by using cultural tools and support from adults to jointly problem solve (Rogoff et al., 1993). The guidance from adults therefore becomes an essential element for joint problem solving and decision making. The opportunities for joint work are easy to realise in locales where children spend most of their time, which generally are at home and/or in school. These locales hence have a huge influence on how their rights can be realised into practice (Deb and Mathews, 2012). Participation, with the guidance from adults in these two locales, therefore, can increase children's capacity to think rationally and critically, both individually and in group situations.

Guided participation can easily be confused with socialisation which suggests that children can be trained and shaped through social culture, but this may suggest an element of *control.* The control, when exercised through rigid rules, reduces the chances for meaningful participation (Bae, 2009) and often leads to conflicting situations (Doumen et al., 2009). Attempts must therefore be made to diffuse the vertical wall of hierarchy of authority between the adults and children and encourage and invite them to contribute their views in a non-conflicting environment. This will eventually provide opportunities for meaningful conversation whilst also providing potential for the new learning to take place, for both the child and the adult.

The benefits and implications of children's participation are now being realised and translated into pedagogical approaches while interacting with children. A practitioner is expected to reflect on the child's preferred communication style and characteristics of learning and then recognise how these can be utilised to aid future learning potential. An example of this could be by equipping our learning environment in a way that helps children to first 'form' and then 'communicate' their preferences. An example from Richmond Preschool (in Benfleet, Essex) is discussed below (Box 3.1) where they carry out '*look, listen and note*' techniques (DCSF, 2008a: 5) to help children form and communicate their preference for resources, which practitioners then observe, record and analyse to aid further participation.

Practitioners therefore play a key role in implementing participatory principles into practice. Their role involves not only welcoming parents and families within an early years educational environment, but most importantly, welcoming the child. Sensitivity is required in order to get to know the children as holistic individuals, who should feel comfortable and confident enough to participate through the curriculum provision (DfE, 2012).

Barriers to children's participation in education

Traditionally children have been regarded as passive bystanders in their worlds. Their participation has sometimes been hampered by the view that they should be free and protected from responsibilities of an adult world until they are mature enough to cope (James and Prout, 1997). Adults have a responsibility to ensure that all children are kept safe from harm, but beyond that, adults should enable and encourage children's participation within their environment in a way that suits the child and is not driven by the agenda or personal beliefs of the adult. Adults' natural drive to protect young children can inadvertently prevent them from allowing children's participation to take place (James and Prout, 1997), which at a pedagogic level, can hinder children's learning and development.

Acknowledging what participation can mean for a child is essential when trying to provide an enabling environment. But in order to promote participation in everyday practice, practitioners often face challenges. These challenges may range from a personal attitude towards 'childhood' and 'participation' to the challenges faced by the 'demands of a prescriptive curriculum'. The section below summarises some of the issues and challenges in implementing participatory practices in education.

First of all, it is critical to understand the delicate balance between participation and protection as too much emphasis on the views of children as autonomous and competent beings can make us underestimate their vulnerable sides (Bae, 2009). Bae, on this continuum, recognises practitioners' three different views on children:

BOX 3.1: THE LOOK, LISTEN AND NOTE EXAMPLE

At Richmond Pre-school CIC in Essex we provide children of all ages, stages and abilities with encouragement in accessing resources and participating in their own learning without the added pressure of having to engage verbally, particularly if they are new to the environment and have not yet built the confidence or have the ability to converse with others. We have photographs of resources stuck with velcro, making them movable, on transparent boxes. Children can choose to use the pictures to request items, if that is how they feel more comfortable. We always respond to their request by modelling verbal communication, for example 'Yes, you can have the mobilo', taking them to the box, replacing the picture and getting out the box requested.

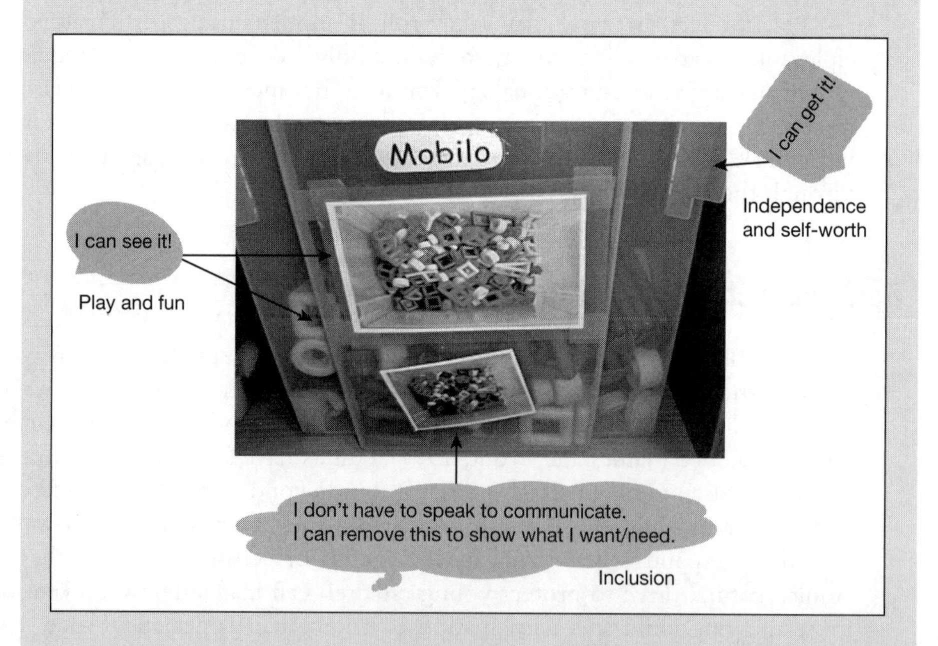

The photographs can be utilised for different purposes including supporting PECS (Picture Exchange Communication System), providing reminders for tasks and helping children to remember what it is they are helping to tidy away. This not only helps children to interact with various resources but also encourages them to participate in their own learning by forming choices and the ability to communicate their preferences to adults in the setting.

1. That practitioners know better than the child,
2. that the child is irrational,
3. that children are fellow human beings.

(Johansson, 2003, cited in Bae, 2009)

These conflicting views about 'children' often act as the first encroachment of children's participatory rights. The traditionalist views (the first two) make us advocate children's voices on *behalf* of them whereas the organic view (third) emphasises the creation of enabling conditions in which a child feels empowered to express his/her voice without being dependent on adults. Bae (2009) asserts that as self-reflective adults it is up to us to alter our attitude if and when necessary, in order to enable children to participate in their own way and in their own time.

The second biggest barrier to children's participation in education is around the simultaneous promotion of independent thinking and attention to children's voices whilst following the rigid parameters of a prescriptive curriculum. The pedagogical approaches to understanding *individual needs* within *group contexts* can create conflicting situations for the practitioner. For example, individual practices might stimulate too much self-determination and individual choice, making it difficult for the practitioner/teacher to attend to multiple voices at one given time (Bae, 2009). Children's participatory rights, therefore, need to be followed with a holistic view that they do not operate in isolation and are best achieved by balancing them with other rights. Bae (2010: 207), for example, demonstrates a link between different articles in the Convention: 'Article 12, as a general principle, is linked to the other general principles of the Convention, such as Article 2 (the right to non-discrimination), Article 6 (the right to life, survival and development) and, in particular, is interdependent with Article 3 (primary consideration of the best interests of the child).'

This holistic and interdependent view can be evidenced in the revised Early Years Foundation Stage (DfE, 2012) curriculum which confirms the importance of 'Communication and Language', 'Personal, Social and Emotional Development' and 'Physical Development' as 'prime areas' of learning and development for young children. Children need to be able to recognise and make social and behavioural connections within a group for participation to become easier (Rogers and McPherson, 2008). It is our role as adults to recognise how each child prefers to communicate (DfE, 2012). We must nurture their preferences while providing support towards a shared communication for all children who attend provision.

A third barrier to participation can be a lack of consistency and continuity between the home and education setting's culture and practices. Flewitt (2005) recognises that children's participation depends on their understanding of the verbal and gestural cues emitted from other children and adults in the provision. To this, Rogoff et al.'s (1993) acknowledgement of the difference in home–setting culture vindicates the barrier to participation. They suggest that if the home culture of the child is different from the setting's culture, for example if it relies mainly on verbal cues, the physical gestures provided in the setting may be missed. The settings therefore need to establish positive relationships with parents by working closely with them and sharing information (DfE, 2012). This enables consistency within children's care and education where settings can understand home cultures and traditions and introduce them, including physical cues, which in turn will enhance relations and understanding for all. An acknowledgement and agreement of expectations therefore should be discussed regularly between practitioners, parents and children to provide recognition and consistency within a provision.

A fourth barrier is the common misconception that children's participation means that a final decision has to be taken by the child. Children's participation must be followed with the basic principle of participation leading to 'action'. These actions can range from a small change to the selection of reading books to a change in the layout of the classroom environment. The aim is to create a shared pedagogical space where learning can be co-constructed, commonly referred to as the pedagogy of 'listening' (Rinaldi, 2001). Participatory processes therefore should have outcomes for both children and adults – adults as co-learners and co-interpreters (Mannion, 2010). Children's participation, as an important aspect of the pedagogy of listening, can be promoted at different levels. It can range from 'giving information' to 'shared decision making and empowerment' (Walker and Logan, 2008) (for details on levels of participation, please refer to Chapter 4). The barrier, however, is when we start looking at these levels in a strict hierarchical order and become too critical of our efforts. These levels are only there to help us determine where we are in terms of participation. Settings can then start from a point that is realistic for them and then develop participation as their collective confidence, trust and skills increase (Ladder of Participation, n.d.). Children's views, as Shier (2001) suggests, are one of the several factors that will have to be taken into account in their education. Similarly, Sheridan (2007) argues that participation is not always a question of leaving the decision to the child but to involve children 'to make them feel that they are competent to participate in decision-making processes by communicating with them, asking questions, listening to them in order to encourage them to develop skills and a desire to argue for their standpoints' (Sheridan, 2007: 204–205).

A fifth barrier to participation is often the inability of the practitioner to choose an appropriate means to document and/or understand children's voices. 'Voice', which is often used as a metaphor for participation, is related to the concept of representation, which is likely to make us think about the structures – the tools that we use every day in the settings (such as a tick sheet, children's assessments, etc.). We do not deny the importance of these tools, yet they predominantly display the structures of policy makers (for example, documentation as an evidence for Ofsted). Porter (2008) argues that structures do not have voices – people do. Structures, though significant in giving an indication about children's experiences, may not necessarily give an insight into the meaning-making process. Attention therefore needs to be paid in using different forms of pedagogical documentation which not only record children's achievements but also describe and give meaning to their experiences. Examples of such processes are outlined in Chapter 4 and can be explored for their use as pedagogical documentation *for* and *by* children.

Considering the barriers described above, it becomes apparent that there are certain preconditions that need to be followed in order to embrace participatory principles into practice. These conditions are summarised below in a list format:

- Give children both a room and space (physical and mental) to be able to make choices and take the initiative
- Develop children's agency over time
- Support them to develop and articulate their views
- Create opportunities for them to discuss options
- Listen consistently
- Adapt decision-making systems to ensure that actions result from children's involvement
- Move beyond pervasive paternalism
- Pay attention towards:
  - What is happening at the policy level
  - How theoretical ideas can offer useful insights into professional practice

(Samuelsson and Fleer, 2008; Jerome, 2011; Bae, 2010)

Non-participation and children's behaviour

While discussing the benefits and preconditions for participation, it is also imperative to consider non-participation in an education context. It often originates from a rigid learning environment, consequently appearing and displayed through a child's unwanted behaviour. These problems can surface when children become frustrated due to being misunderstood (DCSF, 2010). If children feel misunderstood or if they do not understand boundaries or situations within their environment, they may begin to display undesired behaviours. Disruptive behaviour caused through frustration can impact children's emotional development (DCSF, 2008b), highlighting the need to look at the whole situation with a critical viewpoint, not just at the child but towards ourselves, as adults. We must be attentive towards what the children tell us through their physical and verbal responses, so that a shared understanding can be established (DCSF, 2008b). Some adults believe that listening to children who display challenging behaviour can provide a possible imbalance of power (Essex County Council, 2010). These perceptions are influenced by the personal view of children adopted by the practitioner which can open or hinder possibilities for future participation.

Non-participation, other than the disruptive behaviour, can also be interpreted through a child's silence. Silence, often interpreted as disengagement, can be essential for internalising the learning environment which can widen children's knowledge of gesture, speech and expectations and also possibly accommodating new meanings (Silin, 2006; Tizard and Hughes, 1984, cited in Flewitt, 2005: 208). Even the most fluent talkers could be less verbal at pre-school than within their home environment (Flewitt, 2005), as they may need to become familiar with their new social culture. Being in a diverse environment may mean that children could be learning new social mores. Flewitt (2005) argues that children's silences are often ignored by adults, but should be recognised as a powerful developmental tool in preparation for communication (Bruner, 1983, cited in Dunn, 1998: 6) and in turn enabling participation.

In both situations, whether it is a display of disruptive behaviour or silence, we need to 'read' the children's gestures and cues in order to understand them and acknowledge the messages they are trying to relay. We must provide calm and reassuring feedback in a way that we know the child can access, and which can calm the child. They need to feel listened to in order to maintain participation for now and for the future (Hart, 1992).

It is, however, not just the role of the key practitioners to attend to children's views but also the setting's leaders who should be effective communicators too. In order for their communication to be effective, it should be both multi-functional and multi-directional (Siraj-Blatchford and Manni, 2007). Transparency regarding practice, processes and expectations should be provided and recognised throughout provision, including children's learning and development, staffing issues and training (Siraj-Blatchford and Manni, 2007). It is therefore equally important to give opportunities not only to children to participate and express their views but also to the adults who work in that education setting. This consistent approach towards staff and children helps to create a culture of participation. Being a good role model will not only encourage the children to replicate these means of communication but also opens the opportunity for adults to evolve a truly participative environment where all participants' views are duly respected and attended. There may be challenges associated with this due to power differentials and the level of influence different participants can have on the running of a setting. An interaction and alignment of the values and attitudes of all participants is therefore essential in determining the success of any education institution.

Believing in these principles, Jane decided to carry out a staff meeting/training session as the director and setting leader of Richmond Pre-school in Benfleet, Essex. The aim was to consider displays of challenging behaviour by children which may have arisen due to various factors, such as being misunderstood; a lack of their preferred communication style being considered; children testing the boundaries within the environment; or an underlying cause of a pre-diagnosed condition (DCSF, 2010). The training was based on Senge's (2006) recognition that we, as adults, can remain 'fixed' in our views and sometimes require prompting in order to develop them. Staff development thus provided was in the form of a workshop, utilising information from the 'Inclusion Development Programme' (IDP) (DCSF, 2010), making a participative environment in staff consultations and staff meetings. It is described by Jane in Box 3.2 (below).

Empowering children via a 'Spiral of Empowerment'

Cautiousness as to whether children are doing right or wrong may hinder their participation. Merely including children does not ensure that there is a *shared* acknowledgement, contribution and understanding of what is expected by either the child or adult. Over many years of working within an early years environment, Jane began to realise that children ultimately need to feel empowered and when they do, their learning and development seems to accelerate. This happens particularly when they are presented with opportunities which allow them to recognise that they have been acknowledged, heard and understood, through whatever way they have chosen to demonstrate their participation. On occasions, playful games could alter simply by the presence of an adult (Dunn, 2004), particularly if the child senses that the adult is not as playful as they may want them to be or does not approach them in a sensitive manner.

It is imperative to immerse ourselves (practitioners) in analysing what our observations are telling us about the child. Reflecting on our observations so closely is a key element in understanding how the children are choosing to participate. Practitioners must also remember that their participatory approaches alter through various activities and as the children naturally develop. Sensitivity and careful consideration for the child is paramount, when ensuring the sustainability of children's participation. The only way to empower each child through their participation was to develop a 'Spiral of Empowerment' (Figure 3.4) that could evolve as the child's participatory preferences evolve.

An example of how the 'Spiral of Empowerment' was used to encourage a child's continuing participation within Richmond Pre-school is demonstrated in Chapter 6 through a vignette of practice.

Summary and conclusion

We recognise the need to safeguard children within early years environments, although this does not mean to hinder their participation due to the belief that they are not yet mature enough to make their own decisions. We appreciate that the beliefs and attitudes will differ between individuals (children, staff and parents) and households, and we must therefore agree as individual settings as to what our rules and boundaries will be, in order to provide a consistent approach. Failing to provide consistency will confuse the children and will more than likely result in unwanted behaviours. In order to explore the attitudes and ideas that practitioners hold about children, it is effective to provide some training or workshops where practitioners can discuss how they feel in relation to children's behaviour and explore how their attitudes could affect the children in their care. In using the 'Spiral of Empowerment', a clear vision can be constructed of what can be done next for the child in terms of empowering them to feel able to continue to participate.

BOX 3.2: UNDERSTANDING CHILDREN'S BEHAVIOUR

The IDP (DCSF, 2010) provides guidance documentation for practitioners within the early years, promoting inclusive practices. The focus in 2010 was 'Supporting children with Behavioural, Emotional and Social Difficulties' (DCSF, 2010). My intention was to provoke self-reflectiveness in practitioners, taking inspiration from de Bono (1991) when devising the training activity. He recognised that in order to perceive something from the perspective of somebody else we should first remove our own 'logic' (de Bono, 1991). I devised possibilities for exploration but with an insight into the child's possible 'logic' to enable potential perspectives to be recognised. To demonstrate my point I devised what I called 'The child in pieces' (Figure 3.2) and issued one each to all staff members.

We discussed the possibilities of what the child may have experienced by taking off one element within each 'area'. The purpose of the exercise was to enable staff to begin to understand what a child may have experienced that can potentially shape their behaviours. The exercise was imperative to children's participation as children who struggle to communicate their wants and desires will demonstrate their frustration through their behaviour (DCSF, 2008b); although Dunn (1998) argues that displays of unwanted behaviours tend to be apparent when children recognise that their rights are being compromised. Whatever reasons a child may have, we need to understand the child, while remaining open-minded as to how they feel whilst also trying to consider their perspective.

We made up 'one child' (Figure 3.3, 'The child in pieces, a better understanding'). I made references to recognised behaviour traits detailed in the IDP (DCSF, 2010) as demonstrated below in Figure 3.3.

Through group discussion, reasons behind various displays of behaviour grew and caution began to rise when assumptions of reasons were provided. We established that 'The child in pieces' could be adapted and utilised to aid understanding of the behaviours witnessed for our own key children. We discussed the two remaining traits that were not placed within my original scenario of the child within Area 1, being 'very active behaviour' and 'aggressive behaviour' (DCSF, 2010: 11). Through discussion we agreed that the two behaviours can tend to develop through or as a consequence of children being misunderstood, recognising they could be displays of satisfaction or frustration. Acknowledgement that situations can provoke different behaviours developed and potential home related expectations were regarded (numbered statements on 'the child', in Figure 3.2). A joint agreement was established as to how our support and understanding can enable children's future participation when they realise they have been heard and understood (Hart, 1997), irrespective of how they may need to express themselves or behave.

Once the 'made-up child' (Figure 3.3) was explored and the possible home culture regarded, I introduced the three categories of the adult as recognised by Johansson (2003, cited in Bae, 2009: 393). Bae (2009) suggests that discussing staff attitudes to situations can raise consciousness and provoke self-reflection which can encourage meaningful conversation that may provide a self-critical perspective. When thinking about

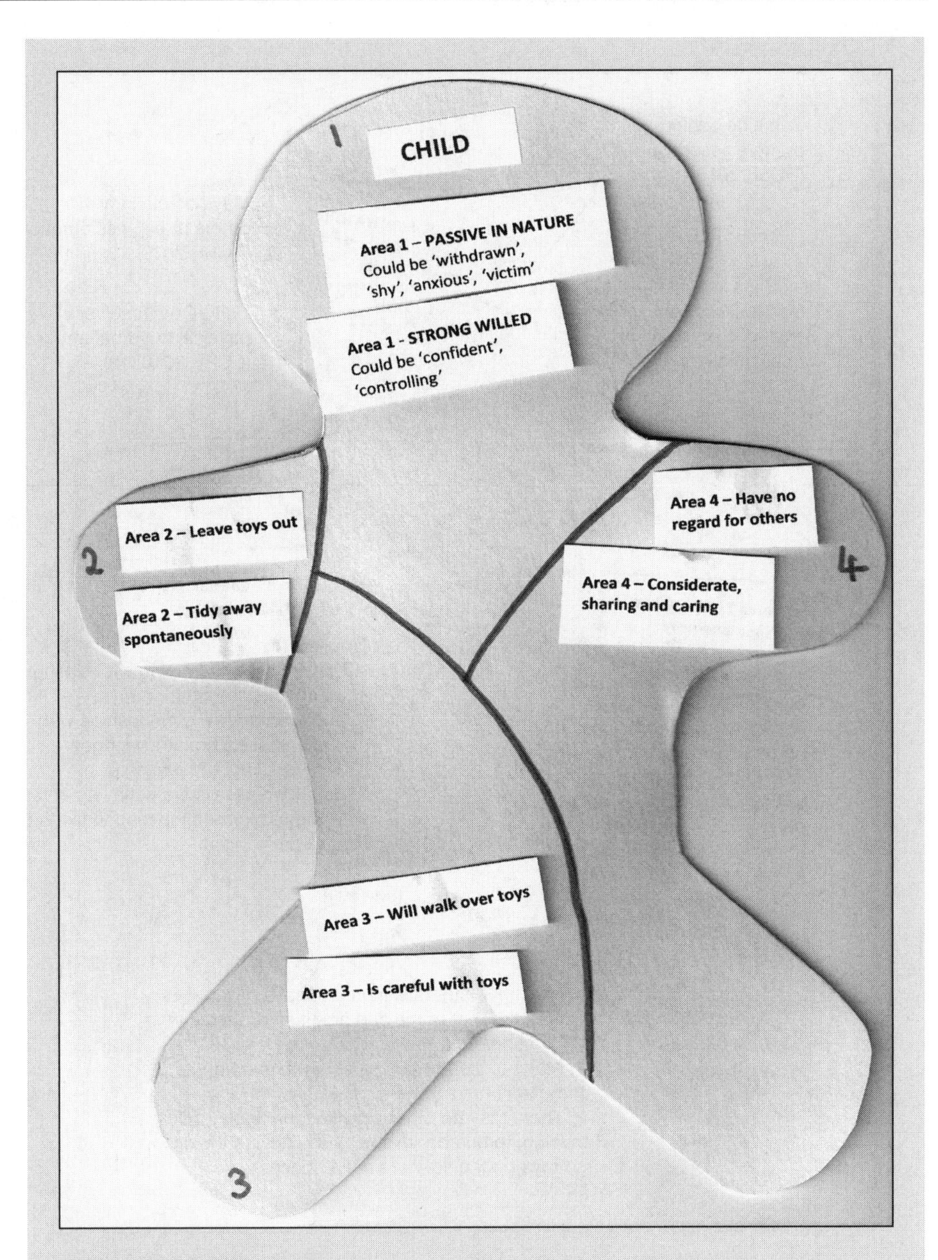

FIGURE 3.2 The child in pieces

the child and their actions the practitioners began to reflect on what their initial thoughts of the action alone would be. This helped them see that their perspective and reaction may not always benefit the child. Practitioners realised they should reflect-in-action (Schön, 1983, cited in Collins et al., 2010: 246), which could benefit the children. My evaluation of the training enabled me to recognise the influence the activity had on

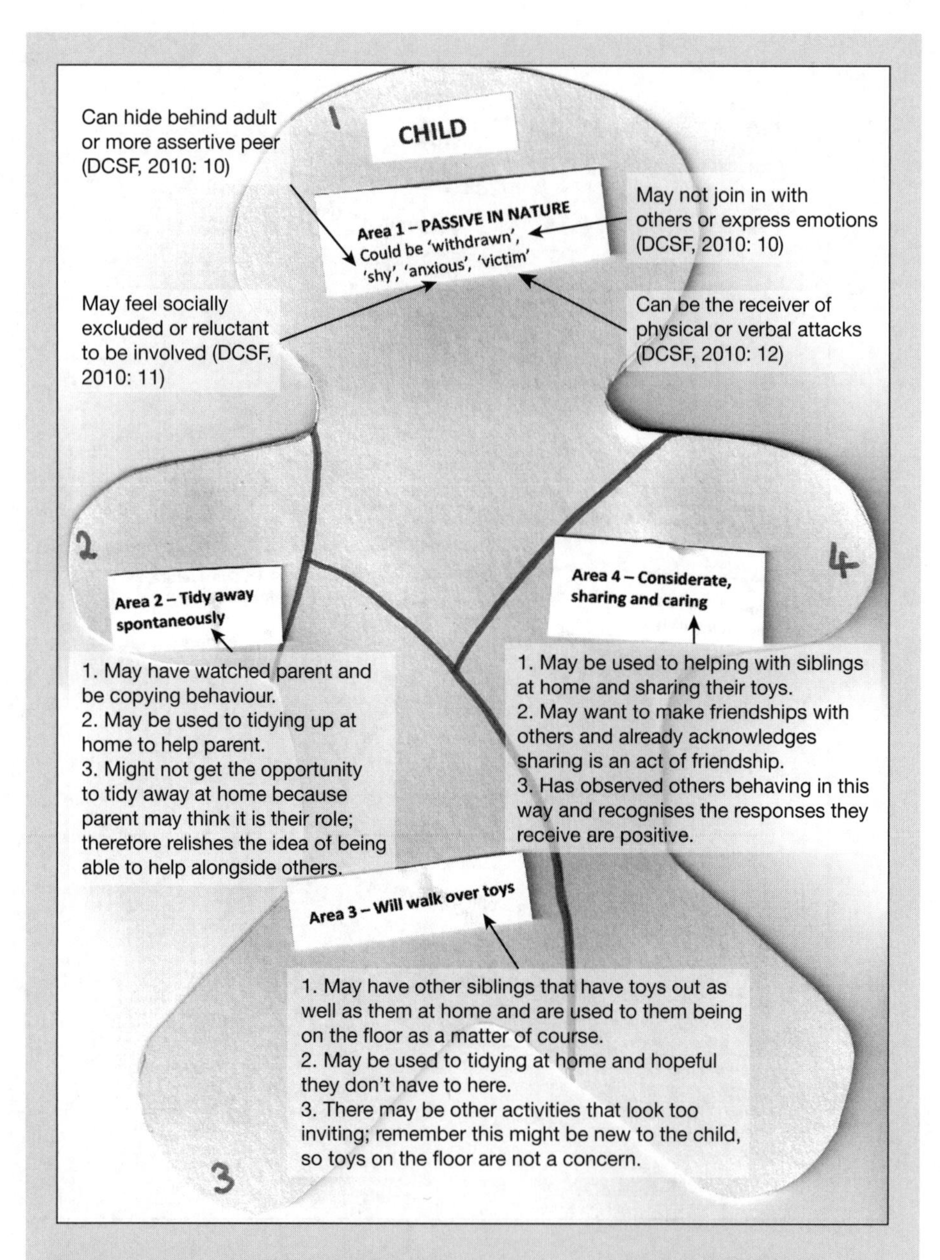

FIGURE 3.3 'The child in pieces, a better understanding'

the practitioners, potentially aiding improvement of provision for the children and also providing a shared understanding of good practice (Siraj-Blatchford and Manni, 2007). An understanding was gained by practitioners that providing a controlling environment could hinder the children's ability to participate if they remained misunderstood or controlled.

A Spiral of Empowerment

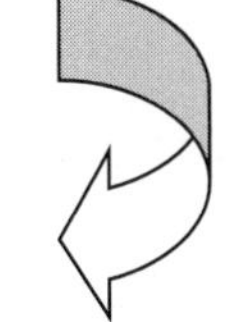

1. Child's words/response/actions
'Look, listen and note' what the child says and does; pay attention to their body language.

2. Reflection – what can be done for the child?
Consider how and what the child is trying to communicate; what their body language is telling you; what are they doing and/or saying.

3. Child realises that he/she has been acknowledged
Directly respond to what you have discovered through reflection; consider how the child could recognise that they have been heard and acknowledged by you and/or within the environment.

4. Benefits recognised for the child
When the child realises that they have been heard and considered, their preferred method of participation will continue to develop and their learning can continue to be extended in ways to suit the child.

1. Child's words/response/actions
Continue to 'look, listen and note' what the child says and does; pay attention to their body language.

FIGURE 3.4 A Spiral of Empowerment

Points to consider and questions to ask yourself

- How can we provide an environment where children can make their own decisions? List some examples.
- How can you ensure that all practitioners are consistent in their approaches and attitudes in caring for and educating young children? How is this consistency communicated to staff and children?
- How do you know if all children feel listened to and valued in a setting? How can you evidence this?

References

Andrews, R. and Mycock, A. 2007. Citizenship education in the UK: divergence within a multi-national state. *Citizenship Teaching and Learning*, 3 (1): 73–88.

Bae, B. 2009. Children's right to participate – challenges in everyday interactions. *European Early Childhood Education Research Journal*, 17 (3): 391–406.

Bae, B. 2010. Realising children's right to participation in early childhood settings: some critical issues in a Norwegian context. *Early Years*, 30 (3): 205–218.

Children Act. 2004. Chapter 31. [Online]. Available at http://www.legislation.gov.uk/ukpga/2004÷31/pdfs/ukpga_20040031_en.pdf. Accessed March 20, 2013.

Clark, A. 2010. *Transforming Children's Spaces: Children's and Adults' Participation in Designing Learning Environments*. Abingdon: Routledge.

Clark, A. and Moss, P. 2006. *Listening to Young Children: The Mosaic Approach*. London: National Children's Bureau.

Collins, S., Gibbs, J., Luff, P., Sprawling, M. and Thomas, L. 2010. Thinking through the uses of observation and documentation, in J. Moyles (ed.). *Thinking about Play: Developing a Reflective Approach*. Berkshire: Open University Press.

DCSF (Department for Children, Schools and Families). 2008a. The Early Years Foundation Stage: Setting the Standards for Learning, Development and Care for Children from Birth to Five. *Every Child Matters: Change for Children*. Nottingham: DCSF.

DCSF (Department for Children, Schools and Families). 2008b. *Inclusion Development Programme. Supporting Children with Speech, Language and Communication Needs: Guidance for Practitioners in the Early Years Foundation Stage*. Nottingham: DCSF Publications.

DCSF (Department for Children, Schools and Families). 2010. *Inclusion Development Programme. Supporting Children with Behavioural, Emotional and Social Difficulties: Guidance for Practitioners in the Early Years Foundation Stage*. Nottingham: DCSF Publications.

de Bono, E. 1991. *I Am Right, You Are Wrong*. London: Penguin Books Limited.

Deb, S. and Mathews, B. P. 2012. Children's rights in India: parents' and teachers' attitudes, knowledge and perceptions. *The International Journal of Children's Rights*, 20 (2): 241–264.

DfE (Department for Education). 2012. *The Early Years Foundation Stage*. Cheshire: DfE.

DfES (Department for Education and Skills). 2001. *Special Educational Needs Code of Practice*. Nottingham: DfES Publications.

Doumen, S., Verschueren, K. and Buyse, E. 2009. Children's aggressive behaviour and teacher–child conflict in kindergarten: is teacher perceived control over child behaviour a mediating variable? *British Journal of Educational Psychology*, 79 (4): 663–675.

Dunn, J. 1998. *The Beginnings of Social Understanding*. Oxford: Blackwell Publishers Limited.

Dunn, J. 2004. *Children's Friendships: The Beginnings of Intimacy*. Oxford: Blackwell Publishing.

Essex County Council. 2010. *I Know I Matter to You*. Chelmsford: Essex County Council.

Flewitt, R. 2005. Is every child's voice heard? Researching the different ways 3-year-old children communicate and make meaning at home and in a pre-school playgroup. *Early Years*, 25 (3): 207–222.

Hamer, C. 2009. The national and international context of listening to babies and young children. [Online]. Available at www.participationworks.org.uk. Accessed March 20, 2013.

Hart, R. A. 1992. Children's participation: from tokenism to citizenship. *Innocenti Essays*, No. 4. Italy: International Child Development Centre.

Hart, R. A. 1997. *Children's Participation: The Theory and Practice of Involving Young Citizens in Community Development and Environmental Care*. London: Earthscan.

James. A. and Prout, A. (eds). 1997. *Constructing and Reconstructing Childhood*. London: Routledge Falmer.

Jerome, L. 2011. Students' perspectives on schooling. *British Educational Research Journal*, 37 (6): 1057–1059.

Kellett, M. 2010. Small shoes, big steps! Empowering children as active researchers. *American Journal of Community Psychology*, 46 (1–2): 195–203.

Ladder of Participation. n.d. Participation – Best Practice Guide: Practical ways of involving children, young people and families in decision making. [Online]. Available at http://www.warwickshire.gov.uk/web/corporate/pages.nsf/Links/1DDB2D17FA6BCBE18025720B003328B5. Accessed August 1, 2012.

Lansdown, G. 2001. *Promoting Children's Participation in Democratic Decision Making*. Florence, Italy: United Nations International Innocenti Research Centre.

MacNaughton, G., Hughes, P. and Smith, K. 2007. Young children's rights and public policy: practices and possiblities for citizenship in the early years. *Children and Society*, 21: 458–469.

Mannion, G. 2010. After participation: the socio-spatial performance of intergenerational becoming, in B. Percy-Smith and N. Thomas (eds). *A Handbook of Children and Young People's Participation: Perspectives from Theory and Practice*. London and New York: Routledge.

NSPCC Factsheet. n.d. An introduction to child protection legislation in the UK. [Online]. Available at http://www.nspcc.org.uk/inform/research/questions/child_protection_legislation_in_the_uk_pdf_wdf48953.pdf. Accessed March 20, 2013.

Papatheodorou, T. 2010. The pedagogy of playful learning environments, in J. Moyles (ed.). *Thinking about Play: Developing a Reflective Approach*. Maidenhead: Open University Press.

Participation Works. n.d. Early Years. [Online]. Available at http://www.participationworks.org.uk/topics/early-years. Accessed March 20, 2013.

Pascal, C. and Bertram, T. 2009. Listening to young citizens: the struggle to make real a participatory paradigm in research with young children. *European Early Childhood Education Research Journal*, 17 (2): 249–262.

Percy-Smith, B. and Thomas, N. 2010. *A Handbook of Children and Young People's Participation: Perspectives from Theory and Practice*. Abingdon: Routledge.

Porter, A. 2008. The importance of the learner voice. *Brookes eJournal of Learning and Teaching*, 2 (3). [Online]. Available at http://bejlt.brookes.ac.uk/article/the_importance_of_the_learner_voice/. Accessed February 3, 2012.

Rinaldi, C. 2001. The pedagogy of listening: the listening perspective from Reggio Emilia. *Innovations in Early Education: The International Reggio Exchange*, 8 (4), 1–4. [Online]. Available at http://academic.udayton.edu/JamesBiddle/Pedagogy%20of%20Listening.pdf. Accessed April 25, 2012.

Rogers, B. and McPherson, E. 2008. *Behaviour Management with Young Children*. London: Sage Publications.

Rogoff, B., Mistry, J., Göncü, A. and Mosier, C. 1993. Guided participation in cultural activity by toddlers and caregivers. *Monographs of the Society for Research in Child Development*. Serial no. 236, 58 (8): 1–179.

Samuelsson, I. P. and Fleer, M. (eds). 2008. *Play and Learning in Early Childhood Settings: International Perspectives*. New York: Springer Verlag.

Senge, P. M. 2006. *The Fifth Discipline: The Art and Practice of the Learning Organisation*. London: Random House.

Sheridan, S. 2007. Dimensions of pedagogical quality in pre-school. *International Journal of Early Years Education*, 15 (2): 197–217.

Shier, H. 2001. Pathways to participation: openings, opportunities and obligations. *Children and Society*, 15 (2): 107–117.

Silin, J. G. 2006. Who can speak? Silence, voice and pedagogy, in Nicola Yelland (ed.). *Critical Issues in Early Childhood Education*. Berkshire: Open University Press.

Siraj-Blatchford, I. and Manni, L. 2007. *Effective Leadership in the Early Years Sector: The ELEYS Study. Issues in Practice*. London: Institute of Education.

United Nations. 1989. United Nations Convention on the Rights of the Child. [Online]. Available at http://www.unicef.org/rightsite/237_202.htm. Accessed June 1, 2010.

United Nations Committee on the Rights of the Child. 2005. General Comment No. 7: Implementing Child Rights in Early Childhood. [Online]. Available at http://www2.ohchr.org/english/bodies/crc/docs/AdvanceVersions/GeneralComment7Rev1.pdf. Accessed December 9, 2011.

Walker, L. and Logan, A. 2008. Learner engagement: a review of learner voice initiatives across the UK's education sectors. *Future Lab Report*. [Online]. Available at http://archive.futurelab.org.uk/resources/documents/other_research_reports/Learner_Engagement.pdf. Accessed July 25, 2012.

Terminology explained

Culture of participation: The development of a culture where *all* participants respect and adopt participatory practices and develop more egalitarian ways of working. It focuses on the development of democratic relationships not only between an adult and child but also on a child–child and adult–adult basis.

Guided participation: A term introduced by the neo-Vygotskian, Barbara Rogoff, within the framework of socio-cultural theory. It refers to a process by which children learn through their participation and interaction in meaningful activities alongside adults/more experienced peers. It refers to children's active and adults' complementary role in supporting children's learning and development.

Pedagogical documentation: This is more than a record of everyday activity with children. It includes documentation of children's achievements in the form of visible records, such as photos, videos, artefacts, children's work, etc., which enable the practitioners to discuss, interpret and reflect on children's learning and their own learning about the children. Gunilla Dahlberg, Peter Moss and Alan Pence write extensively about pedagogical documentation and refer to it as a tool for reflection on pedagogical practice. In a Reggio Emilia early education context, teachers make a record of children's work and other events in the life of the setting as a tool for further research to support reflective practice. They regard it as a process of co-construction amongst children and teachers.

Pedagogy of 'listening': A term introduced by Carla Rinaldi, in the context of the Reggio Emilia approach to early education, in northern Italy. It underpins the pedagogy of relationships, i.e. our relationship with the physical and social environment. It involves search for meaning and understanding through listening, not only to children's and teachers' views but also to parents and the wider community.

Socialisation: A term generally used by sociologists which refers to the process of acquiring social and cultural norms of the society where we live and grow.

CHAPTER

4 Models of participation

Mallika Kanyal

Aims of the chapter

1. To showcase various models and approaches that can be used in participatory work with children (and adults).
2. To consider the theoretical and practical aspects of these models.
3. To analyse the implications of participatory processes on reflexive practice.

Introduction

Participation, as discussed in Chapter 2, is a complex phenomenon and its application leads to challenging implications, especially with regards to the growing recognition of children as social actors, consumers of services and as rights bearers. Its application in an education and care context is multifaceted and can be realised in a range of ways through various approaches. These approaches can be explained through different models, which are presented here as theoretical and practical models. The divide is only to appreciate the different aspects of participation, otherwise the two overlap. They are presented in a chronological order to acknowledge the progressive conceptualisation of 'participation'. The aim of the chapter is to make us aware of the approaches that we can adopt to promote children's active participation as well as to help us identify non-participation in our practice.

Theoretical models of participation

These models help to explain the basic theory behind participation. It is necessary to understand how the theoretical frameworks have been constructed as it helps in developing our understanding of the complex nature of participation (Kellett, 2010). Through these models we are able to understand the reasoning and approaches that may be adopted to promote and realise participation in a range of services, including education.

Model 1: Ladder of Citizen Participation (Arnstein, 1969)

Sherry Arnstein's model is one of the classic theories of participation. It is not specifically related to children but can be applied in a variety of contexts. Arnstein makes specific link to 'citizen' participation and believes that citizen participation is citizen power. Her model of a ladder demonstrates varying degrees of participation, ranging from the bottom rung of manipulation to the top rung of citizen control (Figure 4.1). She believes that participation cannot be achieved without sharing and re-distributing power (Participation Models, 2011).

Barber (2007) affirms the accessibility of Arnstein's model as it gives a sense of gradations in participation, which he regards as a useful starting point for developing genuine partnerships. The critique, however, is the assumption that it may seem to make progression from one stage to another. Children's participation, for example, can be more dynamic and unpredictable than the different rungs of the ladder. Also, there is an assumption that the bottom rungs of the ladder demonstrate inferior participation as compared to the top rungs (Barber, 2007).

Arnstein (1969) was aware of the oversimplified presentation of participation but used it for illustration purpose only. She suggested that the actual division between the powerless citizens and the power-holders is not that distinct. They are not as homogeneous as they may appear in the illustration. She, however, asserted that in most cases, that is how each group views each other. There is also a lack of analysis on the barriers to participation – from both sides – which can range from racism, paternalism and the resistance to distribute power from the power-holders, to poor socio-economic infrastructure, knowledge base and accountability from the citizen groups (Arnstein, 1969).

Model 2: Ladder of Participation (Hart, 1992)

The most common and popular of all models in participation is the Roger Hart Ladder of Participation (Figure 4.2), which is an adaptation of Arnstein's model. Hart also presents participation in the form of a ladder but describes the bottom three rungs as non-participation and the top five as different degrees of participation. This model can help us evaluate whether young children are being manipulated or really encouraged to participate. It is therefore mostly recognised as a powerful evaluation tool but the general criticism is around the implicit sequential nature of the model which can be considered as demonstrating a hierarchy of values (Kellett, 2010).

The model helps to distinguish between participation and non-participation as the bottom three rungs (manipulation, decoration and tokenism) are equally as important to understanding real participation as the top five. Practitioners especially have found it useful to recognise and gradually eliminate these forms of participation from their own practice (Shier, 2001).

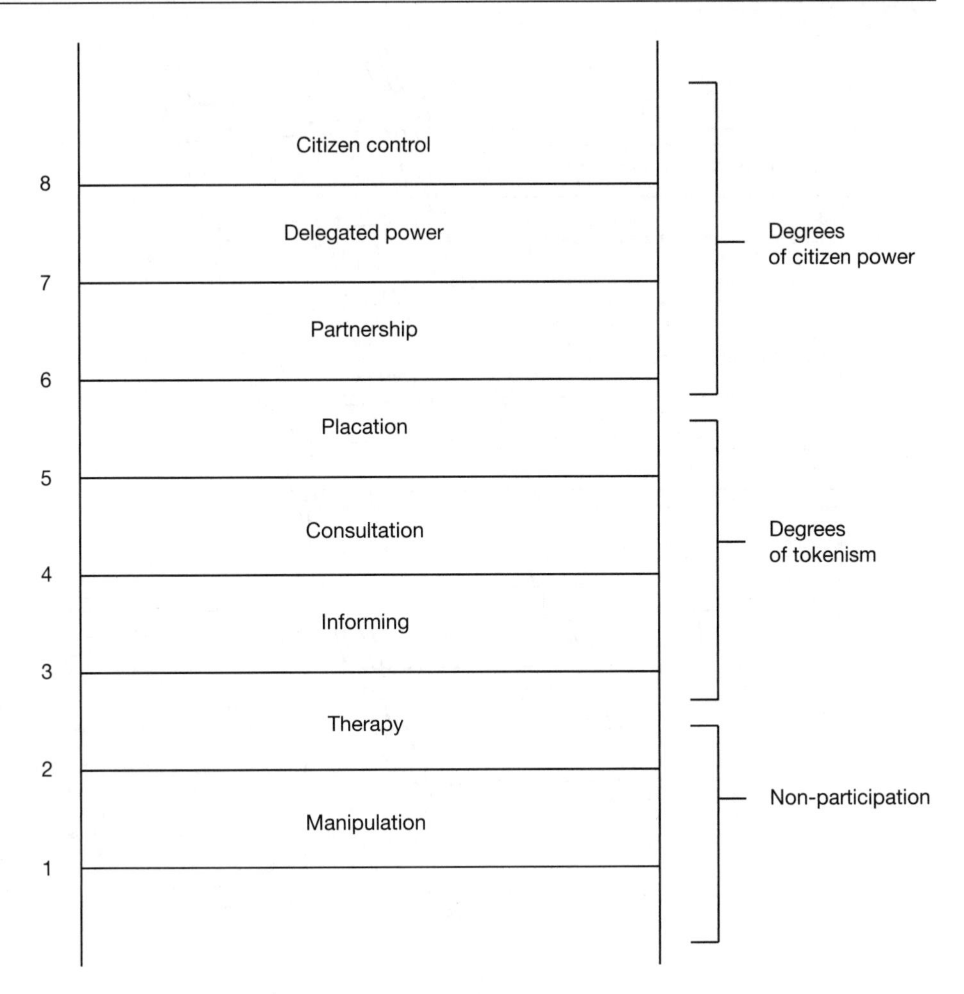

FIGURE 4.1 Arnstein's 'Ladder of Citizen Participation'

Taken from Arnstein, S. 1969. A ladder of citizen participation. *Journal of American Institute of Planners*, 35 (4): 217.

Arnstein (1969) and Barber's (2007) explanation of the various rungs of the ladder:

Rung 8. **Citizen control**: power and control given to citizens. They have full managerial power.

Rung 7. **Delegated power**: citizens given a majority of decision-making seats.

Rung 6. **Partnership**: planning and decision making is shared. Citizens can engage, negotiate and trade off with traditional power-holders.

Rung 5. **Placation**: tokenistic exercises, some public representation and advice in official committees but no real intent to redistribute power or resources. The power-holders have the continued power to decide.

Rung 4. **Consultation**: a step towards full participation but no guarantee that ideas will get translated into actions; hence no assurance of changing the status quo.

Rung 3. **Informing**: a precursor to full participation but can often be uni-directional.

Rung 2. **Therapy**: citizens joining groups to share their experiences – often leads to little social change. Power-holders believed to 'educate' or 'cure' the participants.

Rung 1. **Manipulation**: mere appearance of consultation and participation.

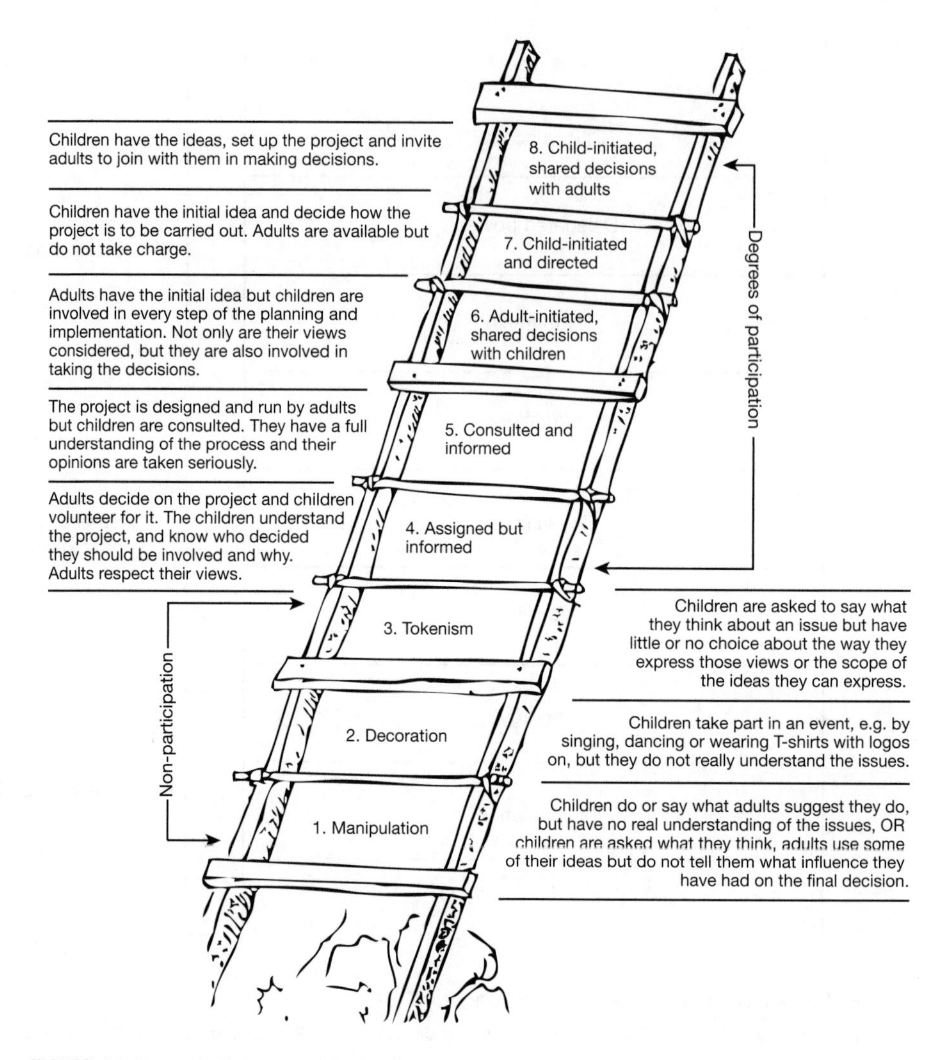

FIGURE 4.2 Roger Hart's Ladder of Participation

Taken from Shier, H. 2001. Pathways to participation: openings, opportunities and obligations. *Children and Society*, 15 (2): 109.

Model 3: Degrees of Participation (Treseder, 1997)

Phil Treseder recognises the value of Hart's model of participation but criticises the assumption of participation as a progressive hierarchy. He argues that the representation of participation in the form of a 'ladder' demonstrates that the top rung of the ladder is the ultimate goal of participation and that it should be the eventual aim of all participatory work. The other rungs are assumed as 'steps' on the way to the eventual goal (McCarry, 2012). Treseder also notes its failure to acknowledge cultural contexts (Kellett, 2010). He therefore proposed a model of 'Degrees of Participation', in 1997, where he recognises five levels of

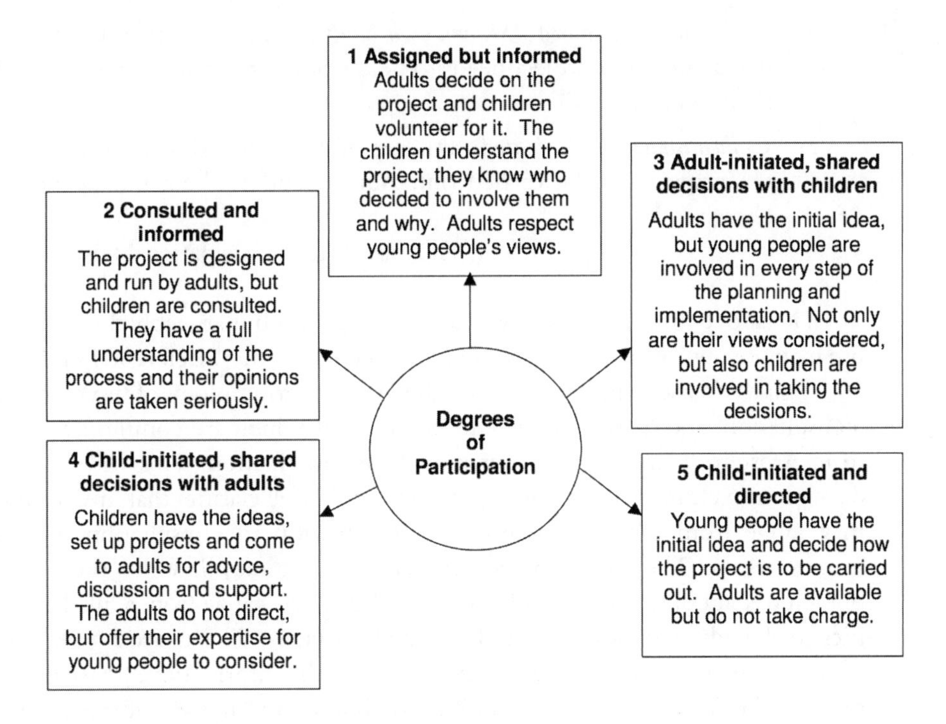

FIGURE 4.3 Treseder's model of 'Degrees of Participation'

Taken from Participation Models. 2011. Citizens, Youth, Online. [Online]. Available at http://www.nonformality.org/wp-content/uploads/2011/07/Participation-Models-20110703.pdf, p. 7. Accessed September 10, 2012.

involvement (Figure 4.3). He uses Hart's top five levels but arranges them in a circular form to demonstrate the parallel and equality among different forms of participation. He suggests that these are different, but equal forms of good participation (Kellett, 2010).

This model shows the non-linear nature of participation. The type of participation is influenced by the nature of the activity that it is being applied to.

Treseder's model represents the following five equally important processes:

1. *Assigned but informed:* adults decide on the project and children volunteer for it. They know the project, know who decided to involve them and why.
2. *Consulted and informed:* project designed and run by adults. Children have full understanding of the project and are consulted. Children's views and opinions are taken seriously.
3. *Adult-initiated, shared decisions with children:* adults initiate the project but children are involved in planning and implementation. Children are also involved in decision making.

4. *Child-initiated, shared decisions with adults:* children initiate the idea and decide how the project needs to be carried out. Adults support and offer their expertise.
5. *Child-initiated and directed:* children initiate the idea and decide how the project will be carried out. Adults support them but do not take charge.

(McCarry, 2012; Participation Network, n.d.)

The above three models appear to have strengths but arguably the terms they use may not appear distinctively different from each other. Bell (2004, in Barber, 2007) gives clear distinction between the generic terminology of 'involvement', 'consultation' and 'participation', the three terms which are commonly referred to in Arnstein, Hart and Treseder models of participation. This will help us in developing a clearer understanding of the models. Bell clarifies that 'involvement' may range from giving and receiving information to consultation regarding specific issues. The extent of power that children may have in the process/ outcome is not defined. 'Consultation', similarly, may range from adult-led activities to the adult support for child-initiated activities. The process gives power to the adults as they can decide what to do with the information. 'Participation', on the other hand, offers opportunities to children to take an active part in the processes as key contributors. They have the power to shape the process and decision making, whatever form this may take (Bell, 2004, in Barber, 2007).

Model 4: Clarity model of participation (Lardner, 2001)

The Edinburgh Youth Social Inclusion Partnership commissioned Clarity (a policy and research consultancy in Scotland) to develop an assessment tool for use by youth workers and young people (Lardner, 2001). This is where Clare Lardner (2001) developed a model of participation by using Hodgson's five conditions for empowerment and Treseder's model of degrees of participation. The five conditions of empowerment include: access to those in power; access to the relevant information; choices between different options; support from a trusted independent person and where needed, a representative; and a means of appeal or complaint if things go wrong (Lardner, 2001), and are expressed in various forms along with different aspects of participation.

The model, which is in a grid form (Figure 4.4), does not suggest participation in a hierarchy, thereby drawing inspirations from Treseder's model of degrees of participation. There is no strict process for its application as different levels of participation may be more appropriate for different situations. The concepts of participation and empowerment are linked to represent the complexities involved in understanding participation.

The grid in Figure 4.4 represents the link between empowerment and participation and 'X' in the middle column shows the degree of participation by

Adult initiated	*Whose idea was it?* X	Young people initiated
Adults decide on agenda	*Who decides what's discussed?* X	Young people decide on agenda
Adults make decisions	*Who makes decisions about how to proceed?* X	Young people make decisions
Adults have most of information	*Who holds the information necessary for decision making?* X	Young people have most of information
Relies on adults to implement action	*Who takes action on decisions?* X	Relies on young people to implement action
Replicates or linked to adult structure	*How formal or informal is it, does it replicate adult ways of doing things?* X	Informal structure and links
Adults have power	**Power shared in between** ←——→	**Young people have power**

FIGURE 4.4 Lardner's Clarity model of participation

Adapted from Goździk-Ormel, Ż. n.d. Have your say! Manual on the revised European Charter on the participation of young people in local and regional life. Council of Europe, p. 108. [Online]. Available at http://www.coe.int/t/dg4/youth/Source/Coe_youth/Participation/Have_your_say_en.pdf. Accessed November 2, 2012 and Lardner, C. 2001. Youth participation – a new model. [Online]. Available at http://www.clarity-scotland.pwp.blueyonder.co.uk/docs/downloads/model_of_participation.pdf. Accessed September 5, 2012.

adults/children. This grid allows for a pattern to be plotted along the middle column which can indicate the degree of control and/or sharing of power between the adults and children. The example above, where the degrees of children's participation are illustrated by an 'X' in the middle column, demonstrates greater control by adults and a moderate degree of sharing of power, specifically for 'decision making' and 'holding information'.

Model 5: RAMPS – A framework for evaluating the nature and extent of participatory practice with young children (Lancaster, 2006)

RAMPS is a useful framework for listening to young children. It originated from the work of Penny Lancaster who developed this framework for the 'Listening to Young Children' project for the Thomas Coram Family, UK, in 2006. It provides a framework for involving children in their learning and well-being, based on the following five principles:

1. *Recognising children's many languages*: children have unique ways of expressing themselves; opportunities therefore need to be given to them to express themselves in multiple ways, for example through drawings, videos, role play and tours.
2. *Allocating communication spaces*: create an environment where children can confidently express their feelings and thoughts in ways that suit them.
3. *Making time*: make time for children to talk and explore. Make time for adults to hear and listen.
4. *Providing choice*: give a choice through different resources, opportunities and routines. Give a choice to children to participate or not.
5. *Subscribing to a reflective practice*: reflect on the processes and share with others (colleagues, parents, carers and most importantly, the children)

(Listening to Young Children in Lincolnshire, 2009; Childwise, 2006)

This is a useful framework to consider before, during and after undertaking any participatory work. The five aspects, as discussed above, lend themselves to an evaluative and reflective tool which can inspire everyday practice.

Model 6: Understanding Article 12 (Lundy, 2007)

Lundy (2007) takes the concept of children's voice much further and conceptualises it explicitly against Article 12 of the UNCRC by referring to four key elements – Space, Voice, Audience and Influence. She encourages the decision makers to focus on these four elements of their provision.

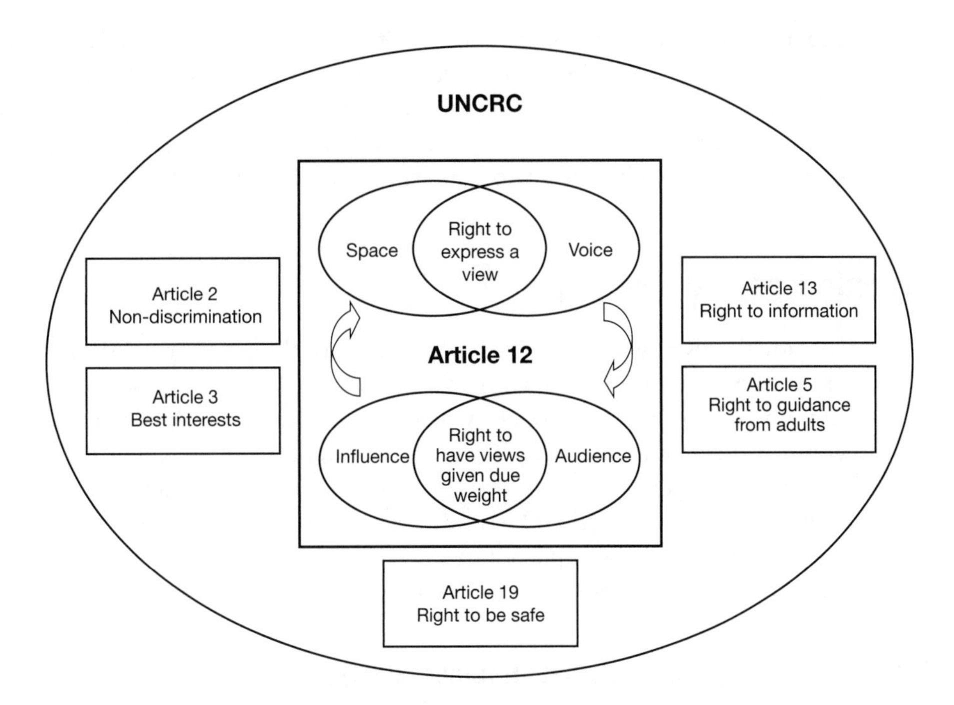

FIGURE 4.5 Lundy's model of participation

Taken from Lundy, L. 2007. 'Voice' is not enough: conceptualising Article 12 of the United Nations Convention on the Rights of the Child. *British Educational Research Journal*, 33 (6): 932.

Space: children must be given the opportunity to express a view

Voice: children must be facilitated to express their views

Audience: the view must be listened to

Influence: the view must be acted upon as appropriate (Lundy, 2007: 933)

The model (Figure 4.5) reflects the interrelationship between these four elements, for example 'space and voice' and 'audience and influence', depicting a chronology of Article 12. Lundy (2007) sees stage one as being the child's right to express a view, then to have his/her view given weight; the last stage is to inform the child of the extent of influence before the process begins again. The model also emphasises the overlap between different articles of the UNCRC and that Article 12 needs to be considered in light of the other relevant UNCRC provisions, such as Article 2 (non-discrimination), Article 3 (best interests), Article 5 (right to guidance), Article 13 (right to seek, receive and impart information) and Article 19 (protection from abuse) (Lundy, 2007: 933).

Lundy (2007) further emphasises the provision of a discursive space for children, for them to be able to experiment and develop their voices. Kellett (2010) supports Lundy's view by acknowledging Lensmire's (1998), Maybin's (2001) and Wyness's (2006) work that argues and affirms the notion of children's voice as a 'project', a 'struggle' and a 'friendly space' which reflects the local needs, interests and children's preferred ways of engagement. Children's voice work therefore needs to be followed with a caveat that it does not become a tool for reinforcing adult governance and equally that children have a right to dissent – not all children want to express a view (Kellett, 2010).

Practical models of participation

The models discussed above are more theoretical in nature as they help us conceptualise the meaning of participation. There are other models, referred to in this chapter as practical models, which help us realise the application of these theoretical ideas into practice. There is no intention of making an academic distinction between the practical and theoretical models and also this is not an exhaustive list of all models. The models/approaches discussed here are the ones which potentially can be applied into education settings. The application of some of the models is explained with the help of case studies below.

Model 1: Pathways to participation (Shier, 2001)

Harry Shier presents this model (Figure 4.6) as an additional tool for practitioners (in addition to the above models, especially Roger Hart's model of participation), helping them to explore different aspects of participation process. The model is based on five levels of participation:

1. Children share power and responsibility for decision making.
2. Children are involved in the decision-making process.
3. Children's views are taken into account.
4. Children are supported in expressing their views.
5. Children are listened to.

(Shier, 2001)

At each level, practitioners/settings might have different degrees of commitment which are identified as 'openings', 'opportunities' and 'obligations'. An 'opening' occurs when a practitioner is ready to work at this level and shows a personal commitment to be participative. It is only an opening as there may not be opportunities to realise this commitment into practice. An 'opportunity' occurs when the conditions to apply participation into practice are met, for example in the form of resources (such as staff time), skills and knowledge (staff training) and development of new procedures. An 'obligation' is established when these opportunities become an agreed policy of the setting. It becomes an obligation on the staff and participation, therefore, gets *built into* the system (Shier, 2001).

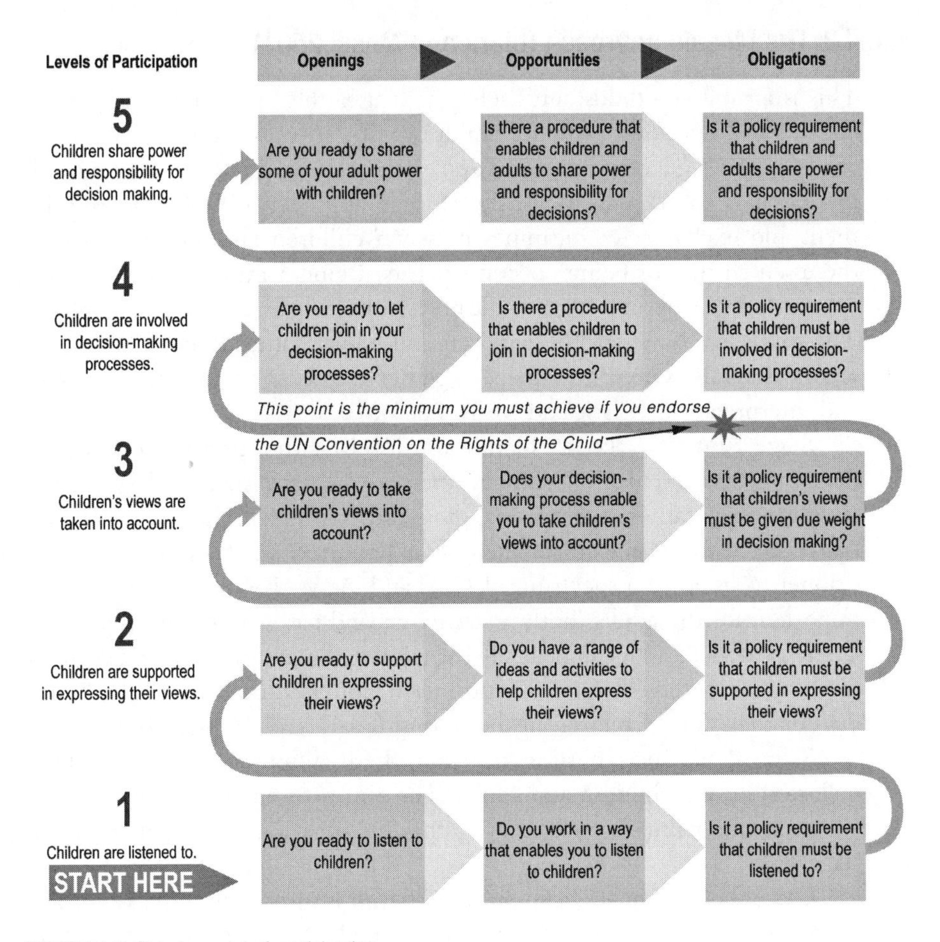

FIGURE 4.6 Shier's model of participation

Taken from Shier, H. 2006. Pathways to participation revisited. New Zealand Association for Intermediate and Middle Schooling, *Dialogue and Debate*, 1: 17.

Shier's model therefore focuses on the role of adults in the setting. It frames participation in the form of questions for the practitioners to consider while planning and/or evaluating their work around 'openings', opportunities' and 'obligations'. The emphasis, however, is on the collaborative activity between adults and children for an effective participation to occur (Kellett, 2010).

The use of this model, Shier (2001) asserts, should not be restricted to a point scoring exercise. If the answer to any of the questions in the model is 'no', practitioners should explore all possibilities of changing it to a 'yes' by probing questions such as 'What do we need to do in order to answer "yes"?'; 'Can we make these changes?'; 'Are we prepared for the consequences?' He proposes the use of the model as a useful first stage in developing an action plan to enhance children's participation (Shier, 2001: 116).

Model 2: The Mosaic approach (Clark and Moss, 2001)

This is a multi-methods approach which uses the 'spoken words' with 'visual' and 'verbal' cues and provides children with an opportunity to express themselves in a range of symbolic ways, such as through the use of photographs or drawings (Clark and Moss, 2005). The approach is central to the development and exchange of meanings between children and adults and adults play the essential role of being co-constructors. Being a multi-methods process, the approach draws upon two main means of collecting and interpreting information. The first stage is where the children and adults gather documentation and the second stage is where they piece together information for dialogue, reflection and interpretation (Clark and Moss, 2001).

Stage 1 involves the use of various tools to gather information on children's perspectives via a range of symbolic and verbal means, such as observations, child conferencing, cameras, tours, mapping and role play. This gives *every* child an opportunity to participate in their own preferred way(s) and allows the practitioner to listen to a spectrum of ideas and views. Being a shared method, it is important for the adults (both practitioners and parents) to contribute their perspectives as well. This can be easily gathered through brief face-to-face interviews focusing on parent(s') (and practitioners') understanding of a 'good' and 'bad' day for their (key) children in the setting (Clark and Moss, 2001).

Stage 2 involves putting together these different pieces of information collected by the children and adults. The aim is to encourage reflexive practice and meaning making by putting together the mosaic of information collected in stage 1.

Once the mosaic has been put together, it is important to make some cumulative sense of the information documented. The information can then be analysed by children's key persons to identify the emerging themes of children's interests and priorities. A simple table format (Table 4.1) could be used to analyse this information.

The table can help to create a 'living picture' of the child's life in a setting. The table can then be expanded and changed with the child's developing and changing interests. This can be done as a combined activity by involving children in the process. They enjoy putting the pieces of mosaic together and will offer more insights into their perspectives whilst involved in the process.

Below is a brief case study (Box 4.1) where a pair of student researchers, Sarah Thackeray and Rugina Begum, from the Department of Education, Anglia Ruskin University, worked with me in a local private day nursery, Solid Start Day Nursery in Chelmsford, Essex. The aim was to understand children's perceptions of their nursery experiences, using the Mosaic approach. The age group of the children ranged from 3 to 4.5 years. We worked with the children and practitioners for about a month and a half in summer 2011. Before we started any work with children, consent was obtained from children's parents and also from children. Parents' consent was recorded in writing and children's consent

Table 4.1 An example template to analyse the information documented by children and adults

Name of the child	Observation theme	Role play theme	Photographs theme	Drawings theme	Video narrative theme	Theme identified by the key worker	Theme identified by the parent
Various areas of interest (or lack of interest) ⇨ For example:							
Outdoor play							
Sand play							
Water play							
Role play							
Pair/small group play							
Etc.							

was recorded in the form of a scrap book, which consisted of the photographs (of us and various activities that we would have liked to do with them) arranged in the form of a story. Sarah and Rugina would read the story every day and record their consent to participate in the activities in the form of a traffic light.

Our mosaic was constructed by including evidence from the following sources – reading books, observations (tracking), laptop (to show them the photographs and video recordings), document camera (used as a tool to encourage discussion about different learning areas within the nursery), video camera and disposable camera (for children to be able to take photographs/videos of their favourite and least liked areas), children's drawings, park visits and interviews with children, parents and their key workers.

BOX 4.1: BELOW IS A SUMMARY OF THE WORK AS DESCRIBED BY SARAH THACKERAY, ONE OF THE STUDENT RESEARCHERS

The children of the nursery were asked to take the researchers on a tour of their nursery and photographs and videos were taken by the researcher of the special places they liked the most.

Through discussions with the key workers prior to this activity the researcher was able to have a clearer understanding of the key workers' perspective on the children's favourite places. Interestingly, the children chose different places from those mentioned by the key workers and when presented with this information the key workers were able to evaluate their own records accordingly and understand that the whole process had indeed given the children a 'voice' in choosing their own activities.

During the whole process different methods were used to observe the children. Tracking was a method used to observe the children, and one that was familiar with the practitioners at this setting. The tracking sheet is a map of the layout and contents of the setting and observations are made of the child's journey from one area to another during a timed session.

This is a very valuable method of observation as it gives a clearer understanding of the child's preferences and is an activity that can be carried out without disturbing the child. Tracking, as a method, was also adapted and used as a dialogic medium to interact with children. The different areas of the nursery, clicked by children, were organised as shown below to represent the layout of the room. This was done *with* the children and most of them were able to recognise which photograph should go where,

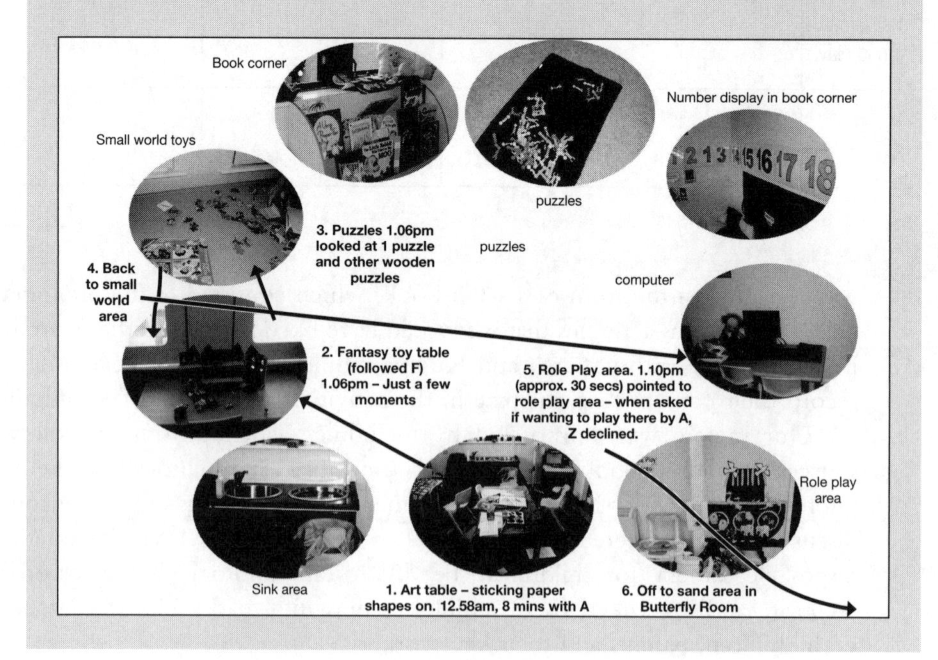

clearly demonstrating their orientation sense. Each child's movements were then tracked and later discussed with them. As the layout was *made* with the children, they were able to connect with it immediately, giving us a detailed account of the activities that they engaged with in each area and also what they enjoyed and what they did not.

The combination of the photographs/videos of the favourite areas and the tracking method illustrate a comprehensive method that can benefit both the practitioner and child.

Another method used was the introduction of a puppet. During our time in the setting, the children were introduced to 'Albert'. Albert is a 'granddad' style puppet who wears a green jumper and brown corduroy trousers and slippers. Albert was very popular with the children and when asked a question by the researcher who was holding Albert, the children would look at him and talk to him. This enabled the whole 'interview' process to flow as the children were asked questions regarding their setting and they would tell Albert all about their favourite places. The children had the opportunity to play with Albert as a puppet but they just wanted to sit him in a corner with a book to read. The introduction of a puppet gave the children confidence to answer questions posed to them and gave them a sense of autonomy as they could dictate what the 'puppet' could do.

The children drew pictures of their favourite areas in the nursery and would show them to Albert, and his name would often be mentioned in our conversations. Below is an example picture that the children drew during the time we were at the nursery. The narratives of their drawings were tape recorded and added to their pieces of mosaics to be discussed with their key workers later.

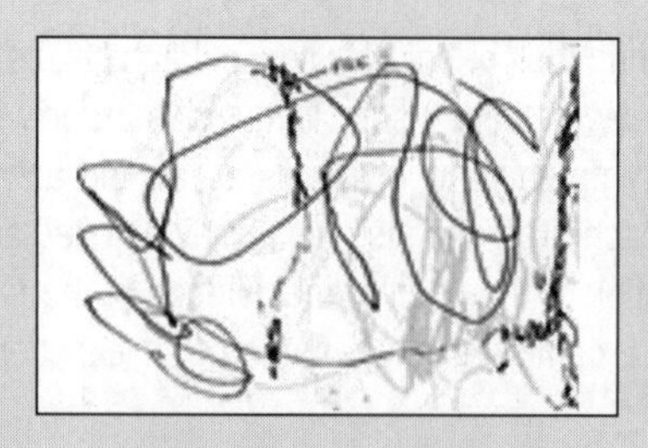

Interviews were also carried out with the parents to understand their perspective on what a 'good day' and a 'bad day' would be like for their child in the nursery. The responses we received resonated with what the children had said about themselves and also with the key workers' views.

In the end, a mosaic was made for each child and presented back to the setting. These were later displayed on the nursery wall, allowing the parents to see their child's perspective of the nursery environment.

By incorporating different ideas and methods, we were able to create a 'mosaic' for each child and discover what *they* like doing and what they would like to do more of. This helped the practitioners to accommodate the children's ideas in the future planning of activities.

Model 3: Cycle of Meaningful Student Involvement (Fletcher, 2005)

This model was developed by Adam Fletcher for the SoundOut programme in partnership with the HumanLinks Foundation (United States and Canada) especially to encourage children's involvement in school processes. It is presented in the form of a cycle (Figure 4.7), illustrating the steps teachers/practitioners can take to encourage children's voice.

The aim of the cycle is to transform children's participation from passive disconnected activities to a process which promotes school achievement and improvement. It is seen as a continuous five-step process which can be applied to assess current practice or to plan future activities. The process is broken down into a cycle with the following five steps:

1. *Listen*: children's voice needs to be 'listened' to rather than just 'heard'. Listening can happen in personal conversations, classroom discussions, agenda items in meetings, or through written reports.
2. *Validate*: this relates to giving feedback to children's views. 'Listening' leading to 'action' is the key. Action/feedback does not necessarily have to be in the form of an agreement to what children say/suggest. A critical discussion about the issues/activities validates the process.

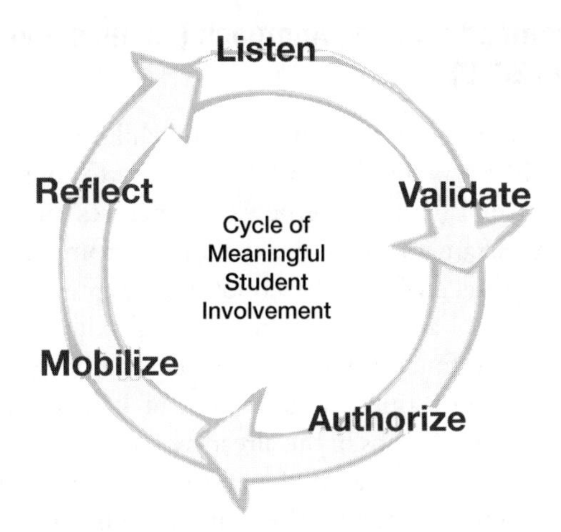

FIGURE 4.7 Fletcher's Cycle of Meaningful Student Involvement

Taken from Fletcher, A. 2005. Meaningful student involvement. Created for SoundOut.org and HumanLinks Foundation. [Online]. Available at http://www.soundout.org/MSIGuide.pdf. Accessed July 5, 2012.

3. *Authorise*: this involves teachers going beyond the traditional role of teachers and giving children the training and positions within the school that would give them the confidence, ability, experience and knowledge to participate actively in various school activities/processes.
4. *Mobilise*: authorising children to new positions gives them a chance to instigate change. Mobilising them from passive recipients to active learners gives them the authority and leadership opportunity to affect cultural and educational transformations.
5. *Reflect*: children and teachers must engage in critical discussions to reflect on what was successful and what was not. Sustaining and extending the participatory experience is equally important and can be achieved by revisiting the first step of the cycle of meaningful student involvement.

(SoundOut, n.d.; Fletcher, 2005)

For this cycle to be effective, it is important that these steps are connected with each other and also with the school improvement plan. It is this connection that makes the partnership between the children and teachers (adults) a meaningful, effective and sustainable relationship. It is, however, vital to keep in mind that participation should not be dictated by adults' personal agendas of performance and achievement. Before getting children involved in these processes it is important to have an alignment of values and attitudes between children, teachers and the setting/school. It is this alignment that will eventually influence the effectiveness of participation.

Besides these theoretical and practical models, there are some other methods that can be used in an education context with young children. These methods are briefly described below.

Method 1: The Diamond Ranking Approach (Thomas and O'Kane, 1998; O'Kane, 2000)

The Diamond Ranking Approach can allow children the choice and control over their learning. It can be used as an effective tool for engaging children's interests by arranging a set of nine statements or pictures in a diamond pattern. The patterns can be arranged in an order ranging from the most important to the least important, thus enabling the children to express themselves autonomously and promoting visual and kinaesthetic learning skills. The nine diamond pattern is more appropriate for use with slightly older children and the number can be reduced with younger ones. The adults can help them create the shape of a diamond and fit photographs in the already created shape. The number of pictures can be increased or decreased depending on the age group and the areas identified and photographed by the children. The activity could be carried out on a one-to-one basis or with a small group of children.

Whilst collecting this information with children, it is vital to be able to discuss it further and understand the reasons behind their likes and/or dislikes. This could help practitioners use the 'liked' areas more effectively for their learning and development and at the same time understand the reasons for children's dislikes. To be truly participative, practitioners need to be constantly encouraging children to express their views about the pictures they have taken, which may sometimes mean asking direct questions. If this discussion with the children leads to any changes, it needs to be communicated to them, thus acknowledging their contribution and encouraging further participation.

When using this approach with a group of children, practitioners can analyse this information to inform their practice. A simple table format (Table 4.2) can give an indication of children's likes and dislikes. Attempts should then be made to identify any emerging pattern/themes and reflect on the use and purpose of learning areas. The following table template could be used to analyse what has been collected by using the diamond approach.

Table 4.2 Analysing the diamond

Areas photographed by children	Number of children who 'like' the area	Number of children who 'dislike' the area	Number of children who are not sure of the area
For example			
Reading corner	III	II	III
Role play area	IIII	III	I
Messy play area	IIII	II	II
Outdoors	IIII IIII		

Method 2: The Magic Carpet

The Magic Carpet is an effective and versatile resource which can be used in a number of ways (Brownhill and Bullock, 2011), for example developing literacy skills and behaviour management. When applied to children's participation, the method can give children an opportunity to go on a journey of their ideal education environment. It can act as a means to open discussion of what they would like to experience within their own settings. The children can sit on an actual rug or a metaphorical one, it is up to them. If using a metaphorical one, they can personalise it by creating a drawing of their carpet that would take them on a journey into the nursery/school world. Different dimensions of interest (depending on the age of the child) could be added, for example how does your carpet feel/look – smooth or rough, bright or pale, big or small? This would not only enhance their imagination but also enable them to create their personal space, taking each child on his/her unique journey of imagination.

Prior to starting their journeys, the children can be shown examples of different areas within an early years setting/school (different from their own) and have a discussion about them with the practitioner(s). The discussion could be aimed at pointing towards the similarities and/or differences in the use of areas and also how it informs children's understanding of the learning spaces within the settings. After this discussion they could be asked to close their eyes and go on their journey (using their magic carpet) of their ideal setting/school. Whilst on their journey they can tell the practitioners what they see beneath them which potentially demonstrates their 'idealised' view of different areas of a setting. Practitioners can use these ideas to inform a discussion between them and the children. The idea is not to change everything as pointed out by the children but to enter into a dialogue with them and make manageable changes once their perspectives have been taken into account. If there is anything that does not look feasible, it should be communicated to the children, with an explanation of the reasons why. This encourages them to get involved in the process of decision making and makes them feel valued and believe that their opinions matter to the adults in the setting.

Box 4.2 shows a case study described by Sarah Thackeray, a student researcher, who along with Rugina Begum used the Magic Carpet and Diamond Approach in a local early years setting, the Solid Start Day Nursery in Chelmsford, Essex.

All models/approaches discussed above may need some degree of familiarity with the methods and/or theories for their effective use, especially if they have not been used before. It may take some time to get them *built into* the provision. As a starting point, curriculum frameworks might offer a familiar context to explore and identify opportunities for encouraging and sustaining participation. In order to give an example from a familiar context, reference is made below to the (revised) Early Years Foundation Stage (EYFS) (DfE, 2012). This is a statutory curriculum framework for under 5s (in England) and all registered settings are required to follow it.

BOX 4.2: CASE STUDY EXAMPLE

The use of the 'Magic Carpet' method as a tool for participatory research was indeed a very interactive experience for both of us and the children involved. To introduce the method to the children we discussed the story of 'Aladdin' (which was a familiar story to the children) and how Aladdin travelled on his 'magic carpet' visiting different places. The children were asked to either draw a mat or find something they would like to sit on that would symbolise one. We used a digital visualiser to project pictures of the nursery and an unfamiliar playground.

The choice to show the outside play area was very important as the nursery has no outside space of its own and the children regularly visit a local park (often daily) to play and have fun. The pictures that were used were of familiar equipment that they would find in their own park. As a result, the pictures created a lot of dialogue between the children and us. The children became excited about going to see their own park that afternoon and were very animated in expressing what equipment was their favourite.

By using this method the children were able to articulate what equipment they enjoyed using the most and that they would like to go to the park every day and play. Due to the nature of the outside space at the nursery, the children were unable to have 'their own' outside play space, but they did not seem too worried as they had daily opportunities to visit their favourite park.

The introduction of the digital visualiser, as a tool, was extremely beneficial for the children, who were able to share different images as well as see various zones of the room whilst sitting on their 'magic carpets'. It was adjusted in various angles to focus on different areas/zones of the nursery room. This instigated further dialogic conversations with the children. It was a great way of showing children that they can visit different places and fuelled their imaginations as to what they could discover in the future. It integrated both a 'visual' and 'verbal' response from the children and resonates with the 'multi-method' approaches of the 'Mosaic method'.

The children were given disposable cameras to use when they visited their own 'outside' space and were asked to use the cameras to take a picture of the equipment they enjoyed the most. Below are a selection of these pictures taken by the children to illustrate their outside play area that means a lot to them.

Later these pictures were also organised in a small diamond pattern by the children (with the help of adults) and we had very interesting conversations about their likes and dislikes. These conversations were noted by the children's key practitioners, who agreed to use them in any immediate and future planning.

The Early Years Foundation Stage (2012)

The key to children's participation in an early years educational environment is for practitioners to recognise the children's likes and interests, and to provide opportunities for them to develop their learning in a way that suits them, without feeling the undue pressure of doing so. During training for the Revised Early Years Foundation Stage (REYFS) (DfE, 2012), provided by the Essex County Council, the tutor displayed how the REYFS fits together in the form of a graphic illustration as presented in Figure 4.8 below.

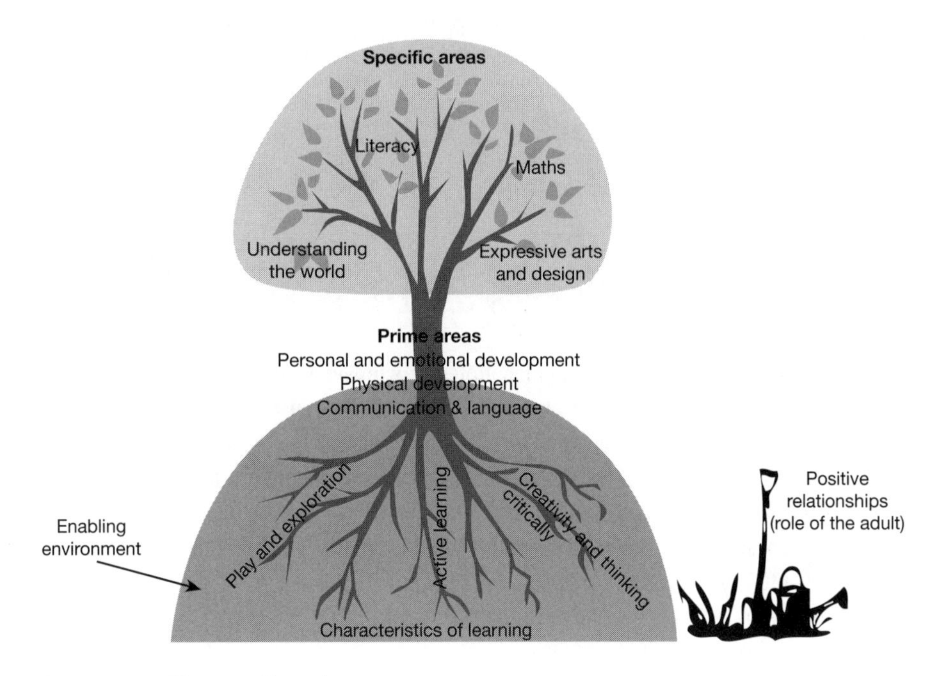

FIGURE 4.8 REYFS graphic illustration

(This diagram is reproduced with the kind permission of Essex County Council.)

Jane Gibbs, the Director and setting leader at Richmond Pre-school in Benfleet, Essex, utilised this presentation for training purposes in her setting. In order to provide effective training to staff, she realised that the diagram would require additional information. Utilising a real scenario that clearly demonstrates the developmental growth of a child and how that happened through the 'Characteristics of Learning', she used a firsthand observation – outlined in the 'Look, Listen, Note' box (Box 4.3) – to prompt discussion on a child's preferred ways of participation.

The example above demonstrates the use of statutory frameworks to provoke thinking and consequently listening to children's both explicit and implicit voices. The boy implicitly showed his preference for a plain piece of paper to a ruled one and explicitly displays his achievement by showing

BOX 4.3: LOOK, LISTEN, NOTE

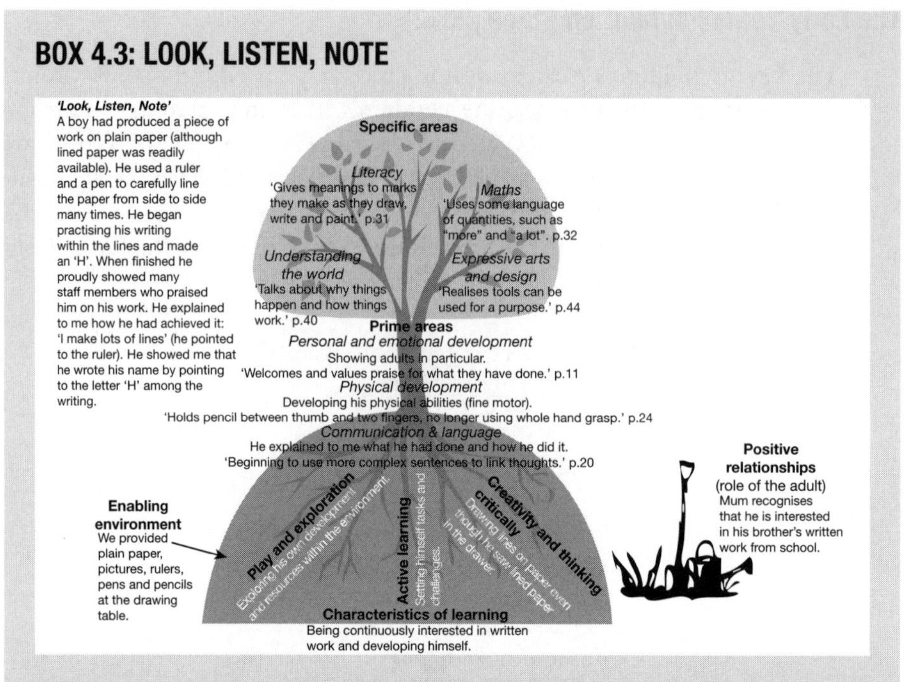

The adapted model (above) demonstrates how providing an 'enabling environment', rich in a variety of resources, for a child who has a keen interest in mark making has encouraged his exploration and enabled him to think critically and achieve new learning. He was very proud of his achievement and keen to show me the lines he had made. I provided wider lined paper for the next time he came in and he began to attempt more letters of his name on it. I can relate this to level 3 of the 'Spiral of Empowerment' (Chapter 3) as he sees the relation with his previous learning and achievement, enabling him to move to level 4 of the 'Spiral of Empowerment'. He began to feel encouraged to write other letters in his name.

it to others in the setting. The recognition of his preferences by the practitioner demonstrates the provision of a 'safe and friendly space' that would enable his development in a 'playful, creative and active learning environment' (DfE, 2012).

Reflexivity: children's participation informing our professional practice

A consistent use of participatory approaches offers a good opportunity for reflective practice. These processes and/or outcomes (for example, documentation) lend themselves not only to analysing and understanding children's perspectives but also to developing a narrative for self-reflexivity. I would like to elaborate on this using Dhalberg et al.'s (2006) analogy of reflexivity. Dhalberg et al. (2006) argue that documentation (which in this instance is about children's participation) may not always reflect a true reality. If adults choose what they want to represent for a child, that means they are constructing the child and this construction is often shaped by the wider social and cultural beliefs of the communities to which they belong. Therefore, while making meaning and presenting that meaning, we inadvertently become the co-constructors and co-producers (Dhalberg et al., 2006). The process leads to our construction as pedagogues and the awareness that we construct about the child often leads to introspection (Dhalberg et al., 2006). During this process of construction and reconstruction we might have moments when we become critical about the dominant discourses of pedagogy and start challenging our own assumptions and attitudes. This stage of interrogation and debate opens up multiple perspectives, showing the metacognitive aspect of participatory practice.

Engagement with children's participation and an acknowledgement of participatory principles, therefore, can lead to the development of an alternative pedagogy. The process of self-reflexivity thus helps in evolving our own philosophy of education, which is informed by the critical thinking and discussions that we would have had at both personal (intra) and social (inter) levels. This way, the narrative of self-reflexivity can be seen as emancipatory, not only for the child, but also for adults as we can free ourselves from dominant discourses of power and understandings and develop our own alternative pedagogies which potentially can be morally and ethically more satisfying.

The methods, as outlined in the chapter, can therefore render themselves to offering critical insight into the role and attitudes of an adult in an education setting. They can offer opportunities to challenge some of the preconceived ideas of being an 'adult', especially the notions associated with the traditional role of a teacher. These are the implicit aspects of practice which often go unnoticed and reflected upon. Therefore the use of participatory approaches is restricted not only to informing planning and delivery of the curriculum but also to understanding/evolving our own personal philosophy of education.

Summary and conclusion

The chapter discusses the theory behind participation through various models and approaches of participation. It gives examples of how these models could be used to conceptualise participation and also how they could be applied in practice. The application is believed to encourage reflexivity by not only reflecting on children's participation but also by reflecting and contesting early years pedagogy, in general. The principles could be applied to challenge power differentials and develop more egalitarian ways of working, contributing to a pedagogy that respects children and therefore their participation in education.

Points to consider and questions to ask yourself

- Which model appeals to you the most and why? How can it be helpful in your context?
- Which method/model could help practitioners start building a culture of participation within a setting? How can it get built-in within the system?
- How does the application of these models make a practitioner co-constructor or a learner? How can it influence practice?
- What challenges can you anticipate in applying these models to practice? How can you ameliorate them?

References

Arnstein, S. 1969. A ladder of citizen participation. *Journal of the American Institute of Planners*, 35 (4): 216–224. [Online]. Available at http://www.planning.org/pas/memo/2007/mar/pdf/JAPA35No4.pdf. Accessed July 10, 2012.

Barber, T. 2007. 'Choice, Voice and Engagement': an exploration of models and methods which promote active youth citizenship in the new Europe. *Planning*, 35 (4): 216–224.

Brownhill, S. and Bullock, E. 2011. *A Quick Guide to Behaviour Management in the Early Years*. London: Sage Publications Limited.

Childwise. 2006. Listening to families. The new childcare act and what it means for you. [Online]. Available at http://www.daycaretrust.org.uk/data/files/Information_Services/childwise/childwise_issue_24.pdf. Accessed November 5, 2012.

Clark, A. and Moss, P. 2001. *Listening to Young Children: The Mosaic Approach*. London: National Children's Bureau for the Joseph Rowntree Foundation.

Clark, A. and Moss, P. 2005. *Spaces to Play: More Listening to Young Children Using the Mosaic Approach*. London: National Children's Bureau.

Dahlberg, G., Moss, P. and Pence, A. 2006. Pedagogical documentation: a practice for reflection and democracy, in *Beyond Quality in Early Childhood Education and Care: Languages of Evaluation* (2nd edn). London: Routledge.

DfE (Department for Education). 2012. *The Early Years Foundation Stage*. Cheshire: DfE.

Fletcher, A. 2005. Meaningful student involvement. Created for SoundOut.org and HumanLinks Foundation. [Online]. Available at http://www.soundout.org/MSIGuide.pdf. Accessed July 5, 2012.

Goździk-Ormel, Ż. n.d. Have your say! Manual on the revised European Charter on the participation of young people in local and regional life. Council of Europe, p. 108. [Online]. Available at http://www.coe.int/t/dg4/youth/Source/Coe_youth/Participation/Have_your_say_en.pdf. Accessed November 2, 2012.

Hart, R. A. 1992. Children's participation: from tokenism to citizenship. *Innocenti Essays*, No. 4. Italy: International Child Development Centre.

Kellett, M. 2010. Small shoes, big steps! Empowering children as active researchers. *American Journal of Community Psychology*, 46: 195–203.

Lancaster, P. 2006. RAMPS: A framework for listening to young children, in Listening to Young Children in Lincolnshire. 2009. [Online]. Available at http://www.ncb.org.uk/media/74676/listening_to_young_children_booklet.pdf. Accessed November 1, 2012.

Lardner, C. 2001. Youth participation – a new model. [Online]. Available at http://www.clarity-scotland.pwp.blueyonder.co.uk/docs/downloads/model_of_participation.pdf. Accessed September 5, 2012.

Listening to Young Children in Lincolnshire. 2009. [Online]. Available at http://www.ncb.org.uk/media/74676/listening_to_young_children_booklet.pdf. Accessed November 1, 2012.

Lundy, L. 2007. 'Voice' is not enough: conceptualising Article 12 of the United Nations Convention on the Rights of the Child. *British Educational Research Journal*, 33 (6): 927–942.

McCarry, M. 2012. Who benefits? A critical reflection of children and young people's participation in sensitive research. *International Journal of Social Research Methodology*, 15 (1): 55–68.

O'Kane, C. 2000. The development of participatory techniques: facilitating children's views about decisions which affect them, in P. Christensen and A. James (eds). *Research with Children: Perspectives and Practices*. London: Falmer Press.

Participation Models. 2011. Citizens, Youth, Online. [Online]. Available at http://www.nonformality.org/wp-content/uploads/2011÷07/Participation-Models-20110703.pdf, p. 7. Accessed September 10, 2012.

Participation Network. n.d. Supporting the public sector to engage children and young people. [Online]. Available at http://part.killercontent.net/media/ae4d430e7a5d4ff886c86b09c19007c0models%20of%20participation.pdf. Accessed July 10, 2012.

Shier, H. 2001. Pathways to participation: openings, opportunities and obligations. *Children and Society*, 15 (2): 107–117.

Shier, H. 2006. Pathways to participation revisited. New Zealand Association for Intermediate and Middle Schooling, *Dialogue and Debate*, 1: 14–19. [Online]. Available at http://www.harryshier.comxa.com/docs/Shier-Pathways_to_Participation_Revisited_NZ2006.pdf. Accessed August 12, 2012.

SoundOut. n.d. Cycle of meaningful student involvement. [Online]. Available at http://www.soundout.org/cycle.html. Accessed July 10, 2012.

Thomas, N. and O'Kane, C. 1998. *Children and Decision Making: A Summary Report*. University of Wales Swansea: International Centre for Childhood Studies.

Treseder, P. 1997. Empowering children and young people, in M. McCarry. 2012. Who benefits? A critical reflection of children and young people's participation in sensitive research. *International Journal of Social Research Methodology*, 15 (1): 55–68.

Terminology explained

Conceptualisation: It means referring to the social theory and literature (in any area of investigation) to understand the meaning of the terms to be used in research. It helps to define and contextualise research aims which then guide the research process. Conceptualisation therefore helps to make sense of and bring coherence to related observations/data in research and analyse them in light of related theoretical frameworks.

Discursive space: A space where children are encouraged to not only participate but also experiment with their 'voice' and views. This constant experimentation, in the presence of peers and adults, helps children to *form* a voice which can be further guided by adults to reflect children's needs, interests and their preferred ways of engagement.

Dominant discourses of pedagogy: It refers to the acceptance of a few dominant ideas and theories in pedagogy without challenging their ideological beliefs. It may or may not be applicable in different education contexts but due to its unquestionable status, can influence practice, both positively and/or negatively.

Framework: In research, every study is based on some broad theoretical principles which determine and guide its course of enquiry, such as the methods and approaches it uses to find answers to the research question. This theoretical and guiding knowledge or body of literature is known as a conceptual framework. Most academic research uses a conceptual framework right at the beginning as it helps to clarify and rationalise research questions and aims.

Power-holders: A group of people who hold 'power' and resist redistributing it to the powerless citizens. They may redistribute it at a tokenistic level but nothing real, thereby maintaining their status quo.

Powerless citizens: A term used in Arnstein's theory of participation to refer to the common men who do not have power to participate in decision-making processes, thereby leading to an emotion of 'powerlessness' in relation to the inequalities and injustice pervading their everyday life.

Self-reflexivity: A process where we have a conversation with ourselves based on what we are experiencing while we are experiencing it. It is therefore a metacognitive process where we interrogate our own practice and may challenge our assumptions based on the evidence. In education, self-reflexivity can lead to innovation and a base for developing alternative pedagogies.

CHAPTER

5 Participation in group care contexts

Understandings and strategies

Paulette Luff and Estelle Martin

Aims of the chapter

1. To argue for a place for participation by and for young children who are not yet able to communicate their ideas through speech.
2. To put forward a case for the 'five Cs': child; curriculum; care; connectedness; and community.
3. To explore the building of participatory relationships in support of the care of young children, with reference to Hohmann's multi-directional triangle of relationships, Noddings' ethics of care and Roberts' ABC model of well-being.

Introduction

Most other contributions to this book focus upon children who are able to express their ideas and opinions through speech. In this chapter we consider the youngest children, who may not yet communicate verbally, and reflect upon what it means to listen and respond respectfully to babies and toddlers. We argue that participation for this age group relies upon specific understandings of their capabilities and, further, the centrality of relationships and three-way dialogues between parents, young children and early years practitioners.

The chapter uses five 'Cs' as a basis for a discussion of participation in group care for children under three years of age. These are: *c*hild; *c*urriculum; *c*are; *c*onnectedness; and *c*ommunity. We begin with a consideration of the '*child*', specifically the nature of human babies and their relationships with adult carers. The work of practitioners who care for and educate young children, in England, is guided by the Early Years Foundation Stage framework (DfE, 2012) and the potential of this '*curriculum*' is explored. We then move to define the concept of '*care*', including the model of a care triangle and the possibilities that this affords for participation. Emphasising the importance of tuning-in to the child, ways of seeing and knowing children are then discussed, under the theme of '*connectedness*', together with the coordination of a wider '*community*' to support relational, participatory approaches.

Child

The scientific studies of developmental psychologists, particularly experimental and observational work in the latter part of the twentieth century, have revealed that babies have multiple abilities. From birth onwards, they are equipped to 'think, reason, learn and know, as well as think and feel' and are, therefore, 'human beings in their own right' (Gopnik et al., 2001: 208). This affirmative understanding of the youngest children has important implications.

Babies and infants are entirely dependent upon others, but they are not passive recipients of care, direction and guidance. They are active social agents who seek protection, nurturance and understanding from parents or other caregivers, which they require for their survival, growth and well-being (UN Committee on the Rights of the Child, 2005: 8).

As Paulette has argued elsewhere (Luff, 2009), if babies and toddlers can be viewed as active members of social groups, then this has consequences for pedagogy and practice. The role of a nurturing adult must be to attend and respond carefully and to participate with the child in making sense of the world. This can be viewed as a two-way process, to which both adult and child contribute. Bruner (1972) highlighted young children's eagerness to learn through interactions with adults and Trevarthen (2002, 2004) also describes babies' active seeking of companionship and their participation in reciprocal communications with adults. Parker-Rees (2007) notes the significance of imitative play with babies within families and raises the question of whether similar meaningful sharing of experience occurs as easily in day care settings.

In Trevarthen's (2003) view, not only is the child motivated to communicate and to learn but the adult is motivated to reciprocate in creative and responsive ways in order to teach the child. It is possible to go further and challenge the view of adult as teacher and the child as learner. Indeed, Montessori (1912) recognised that adults learn from observations and interactions with children; regarding teacher training she states: 'From the child itself he will learn how to perfect himself as an educator' (page 13). This shared participation in learning is reflected in the Statutory Framework for the Early Years Foundation Stage (DfE, 2012) where it is specified that a balance should be achieved between child-initiated and adult-led activities.

Curriculum

The Early Years Foundation Stage (EYFS) (DfE, 2012) curriculum is mandatory for all providers of early years care and education for children from birth to age five, in England. Requirements are set out for learning and development, for assessment, and for safeguarding and welfare. The EYFS statutory framework document does not make any explicit reference to children's rights, voice or participation. There is, however, a strong emphasis upon positive relationships. Each child must be assigned a 'key person' whose role is 'to help ensure that every child's learning and care is tailored to meet their individual needs' and to 'help the child become familiar with the setting, offer a settled relationship for the child and build a relationship with their parents' (DfE, 2012: 19).

Elfer (2005) argues that part of the role of the key person is to be aware of the child's point of view and to advocate for the rights of the child. Awareness of the child's emotions can be developed through the practice of close observations. This may serve to promote empathy within the triangular relationships between the child, the key person, and the child's parents and family (as indicated in Figure 5.1). The quality of relationships and interactions within an early years setting are the responsibility of all early years practitioners but the key person has a principal role in establishing and sustaining attachments with their key children, and with the parents and families of those key children. This forms part of an ongoing continuum of care and continuity in the curriculum that is vital in order for very young children to learn, develop and participate to their full potential (Elfer, 2005; Elfer et al., 2012).

Attachment bonds between young babies and their mother or main carer and also with others, such as the key person who may temporarily share the maternal role (Rutter, 1972), are important for survival and for developing skills. It is within these relationships that babies and toddlers learn about their identity, and discover that they are loveable. Thus, the relationships that children experience at home and in other places with other people, such as in day care, may have a lasting impact. Gerhardt (2004) has argued that the level and quality of affection, love and attention a baby receives is essential in all aspects of children's learning and development because it affects the growth of the brain and influences understanding of emotions. Therefore, the reactions that a baby receives in response to his or her early attempts to communicate will affect how that baby then feels about himself, or herself, and may influence the nature and quality of all future relationships.

Researchers across disciplines continue to identify features of attachment, companionship, and social interactions between babies and their caregivers as important for holistic well-being. For example, studies of the early relationships that babies and very young children experience have provided evidence for a model (the ABC model) that Roberts (2010) has formulated to help parents and practitioners to reflect on how they may promote the well-being of children from birth. This model of well-being is significant in that the young child's participation in reciprocal relationships is emphasised. It includes:

- Agency – a positive sense of self, a positive sense of being a learner and a positive sense of influencing what happens.
- Belonging – a strong sense of belonging and understanding boundaries. Belonging is about a sense of identity in relation to other people and attachment to a few very close companions, and security and trust. Boundaries are about respect for companions, knowing what to expect for the routines, rules and responsibilities.
- Communication – with other people and with the world. Body language is the way in which babies and very young children communicate through listening and looking, touching, smelling and tasting.

Physical development underpins this model as the physical potential and capacities of babies to be in and act upon their environment also has an influence on development (Roberts, 2010).

Martin (2013) recognises that the practitioners' enabling and sensitive encouragement allow the children to communicate with each other and with adults. She also recognises the importance of cultural context of a setting where children are encouraged to participate by accessing materials and making choices about what interests them, as specified in the EYFS curriculum (DfE, 2012). Importantly, the children need to be seen as strong communicators and the practitioners should interpret and respond to their visual and physical gestures. This way of thinking about pedagogical interactions can facilitate participation between babies and children.

The ABC model (Roberts, 2010) of well-being is another way of thinking about how participation within the curriculum is constructed. The 'agency' and sense of 'belonging' in the children can be encouraged through interaction. As the practitioner and the child show their interest in each other, to play and 'communicate', being part of a learning community supports their emerging identities. The quality of communication reveals an understanding of how babies and young children begin to participate as the practitioner understands how and why they communicate and learn together with their peers.

Physical development has been designated as a *prime* area in the EYFS curriculum (DfE, 2012) which is relevant for early years practitioners to consider, particularly in relation to babies, and very young children who are unable to use speech. Practitioners can observe and interpret the physical cues that the children demonstrate and offer feedback and invite the child to continue their attempts to communicate. Sensitivity to the babies' style of communication, including their body language, physical gestures, eye contact, gazes and cries, enables more participatory and reciprocal interactions. Practitioners can build their own capacity towards being more connected and emotionally present, trusting the child's perspective. This is important to allow the child to convey their intentions and to understand their attempts to connect with others, including their peers, and enable playful explorations.

Care

In early childhood, the terms 'education' and 'care' have been used both separately and together when referring to services and provision for children. For babies and toddlers the emphasis has tended to be upon 'care' with services provided privately, or by the state, to look after children and thus enable parents to access employment. Recently there has been a positive move towards the integration of care and education (e.g. Kaga et al., 2010) and to transform understandings through a focus upon the ethics of care (Dahlberg and Moss, 2005).

An ethics of care is useful when thinking about the participation of very young children, as a notion of needy dependants being looked after by a competent adult is rejected in favour of the concept of care as human activity. Noddings (2003, 2005), for example, describes asymmetrical but nevertheless reciprocal relationships between an educator as 'one caring' deriving rewarding feedback and motivation from the responses of the child, as the 'one cared for'.

Hohmann (2007) describes relationships involving a young child, parent and early years practitioner as a multi-directional triangle. Focusing specifically upon family day care (childminders in the UK), she acknowledges that these relationships are complex, and may be tense at times. Nevertheless, there is potential within this triangle of care for understanding and building genuine partnerships with parents and for recognising children's agency in reciprocal relationships with adults (as illustrated in the following diagram – Figure 5.1 – and as exemplified in the case of Rex, in Box 5.1).

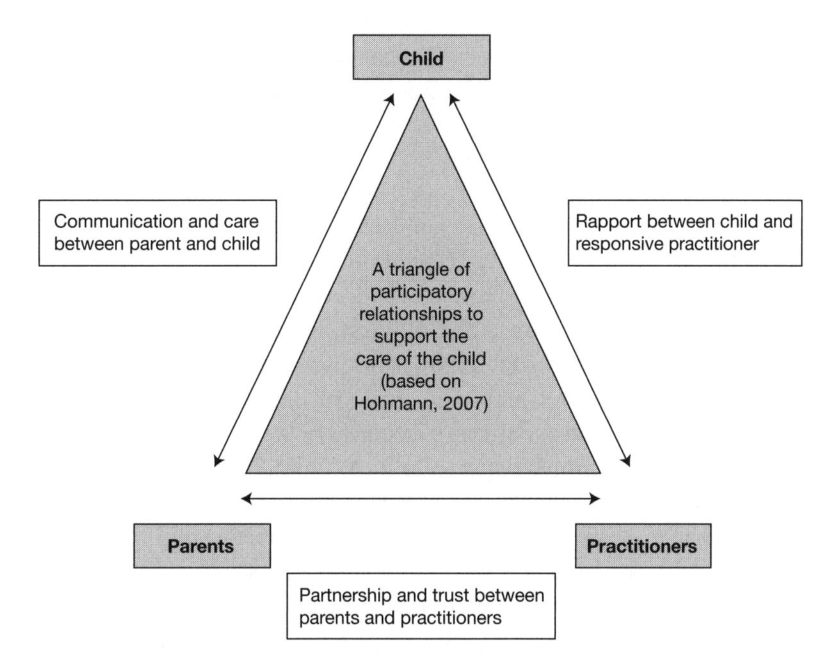

FIGURE 5.1 A triangle of participatory relationships (based on Hohmann, 2007)

BOX 5.1: CASE STUDY EXAMPLE

Exploring perceptions: parents, practitioner, child participation

The perceptions of the parents about interactions between the children and staff were significant because they all had commented on this aspect of the children's experiences as important and described the ways in which they had observed this. Moe, the mother of the child Rex in the baby room, described how staff, Lou and Gerry, had understood his attempts at communication especially as Rex was a late developer with his language and communication skills.

He had developed a gesture with his hand to represent certain levels of pleasure or disapproval, displaying his changing emotional states without language being used. I had observed Rex tapping his head and moving his head to one side, along with other gestures like nodding or shaking his head whilst crying or smiling. It was the sensitive responses of the staff that Moe appeared interested to talk about and the impact that it had because Rex was already managing learning English as an additional language, since that used in the home was Swedish. Developmentally his physical gross motor skills were slow in comparison to other children of his chronological age. Importantly, though, Rex was making multiple attachments during this year with practitioners in the baby room and toddler area, along with his peer group of other babies and toddlers.

So for his mother, the sensitive responses of the staff were essential and acknowledged in the conversations of the focus group. Moe liked that the staff had tuned-in to her child's emotional needs and attempts at communication. I had observed this type of interaction between Rex and his key person, Gerry, within the baby room, where the responsiveness was immediate and Rex had come to trust that his communications and feelings could be expressed. The adult somehow had anticipated and understood his intentions, talking to him about their interpretation as if in a dialogue.

Partnership working between early years practitioners and parents is a requirement within the Early Years Foundation Stage (DfE, 2012) curriculum framework, in England, and essential to the promotion of children's learning and development. As mentioned before, there is a specific focus upon the role of a Key Person, assigned to each child, whose task is to build relationships with the child's parents. There is a responsibility to make information available and to report progress to parents and to discuss any concerns. Parents, in their turn, are expected to provide information about the child, including dietary requirements. There is an expectation that observations and information about the child's progress will be shared, together with a recommendation that parents' comments should be incorporated within children's progress records.

Research on the participation of parents in partnership with practitioners suggests that the quality of their relationships varies. Hohmann (2007) found that the most positive interactions occur when both parent and carer share expectations and expertise, in relation to the child, and there is scope for dialogue and shared decision making. These successful relationships are characterised by openness and trust. Hohmann (2007) suggests that the role that children play in constructing their own care should be the topic for further research. Brooker (2009) argues for a genuine ethics of care for young children, in which practitioners are prepared to wait and to respond to the cues that children give. In this way adults can learn from babies and young children about the care and education that they require. This concept is not new and underpins the approach of Dr Emmi Pikler, in Hungary, developed in the United States of America as 'educare' by Gerber (2002).

Box 5.1 presents a case study from Estelle's research (Martin, 2013) to share an example of how the key practitioners working with Rex were responding intuitively as part of coming to know their children within a reciprocal relationship, which supports communication and promotes a child's emotional well-being through close attachments that are unconditional and contribute to the holistic development of the child.

As seen in the case study example, the practitioner and the child develop their emotional relationship through the active expression of care. The child experiences a warm, authentic appreciation by the practitioner. Identification and interpreting of emotional states requires practitioners to have a heightened awareness and understanding of young children's emotional development and respond to their non-verbal cues and gestures. This was present as described in the case study, as Gerry interprets and responds to the baby's needs and ensures that she lets the child know, through her physical communications, that he has someone there who understands his potentialities and recognises his capabilities. Children learn who they are in the 'here and now' of relationships that enable their participation.

Connectedness

For Noddings (2003, 2005) the ability to be observant and responsive to a child's needs is characteristic of the caring educator. She suggests that caring relations can be the foundation of pedagogical activity and thought. Lilian Katz (1996; Katz and Katz, 2009) also writes of the importance of knowing children as well as knowing about them. One of the 'ways of knowing' described by Belenky et al. (1997), from their research into women's ways of thinking, is 'connected knowing'. This involves a capacity to empathise and understand the experience of others and to know through caring. The sensitivity of Gerry towards Rex, in the case study above, provides a strong example of the connected knowing that is characteristic of sensitive and observant early years practitioners.

Connectedness can be expressed through reciprocal caring, for example through eye contact. A sense of mutuality develops through being together and through emotional and physical connectedness. The child understands that his needs will be met and trusts the person he is connected with. This also links with care, in that practitioners who are responsive to children's needs will also know and understand the baby's or child's intentions and efforts to participate in all aspects of their world. The attachment and companionship reflect the connectedness to each other within a reciprocal trusting relationship.

Connectedness can be seen as a key to participation within day care settings as it can be built between all members of the group. In Reggio Emilia, the view of the child, as expressed by Malaguzzi, is: 'rich in potential, strong, powerful, competent and most of all connected to adults and other children' (cited by Edwards, 2012: 147). The connections that babies and toddlers have with one another are often under-estimated but even very young children quickly become aware of others in their group. The enjoyment and challenge of participation in peer interactions and relationships can be an important source of support and stimulation (Kernan and Singer, 2011). One criticism of early childhood education and care, in England, is the emphasis upon the progress of each individual and the dyadic relationships between adult and child at the expense of fostering group dynamics and positive peer relations (Penn, 1997, 2008).

Community

Children learn to be part of a community of learners when they have opportunities to meet and be with their peers. Continuing studies are informing practitioners across disciplines that children are pro-social and this is highly relevant to children's participation in early childhood education and care settings for babies and very young children. The ways in which adults enable children to engage and participate involves reflective practices and this means that practitioners can review their own perceptions of the ways in which babies and young children communicate and to observe closely how the children reveal their capabilities and intentions (Martin, 2010).

Effective practitioners can be reflective through observing closely and realise that children enjoy being with other children. In this way we can begin to think about creating the conditions for a community of babies and young children.

Planning responsive and culturally sensitive learning for children starts with the relationships that are built with the child and family as part of the community in which the child is situated. These positive relationships, and also the kind and constructive relationships that practitioners model in their interactions with one another, may provide a model for children's developing awareness of others. If practitioners begin to include babies and toddlers in all the activities within and beyond the early years setting, then older children are likely to be inclusive of the youngest members of the nursery community and to allow and enable their participation.

One way in which young children's participation in a wider community may be supported and promoted is through documentation of their learning.

The pedagogical documentation in Reggio Emilia provides an example of this, as it serves as a means of listening to the children and of representing their ideas in public spaces (Forman and Fyfe, 2012). The community is seen as a resource for the children and members of the community may, in turn, appreciate the children's viewpoints through studying the documentation. This approach is sometimes seen in UK settings through the creation of books about activities that children and staff make and share or displays in public places such as libraries.

Summary and conclusion

In this chapter we have explored possibilities for participation for the babies and toddlers in group care settings, through considering the inter-related themes of child; curriculum; care; connectedness; and community. Children, not yet able to speak, are still able to participate, provided the adults in care are responsive to the multiple ways they express their views and choices. A nurturing environment, where there is a reciprocal relationship between practitioners, parents and children, promotes partnership and opportunities for recognising children's agency.

Points to consider and questions to ask yourself

- In your opinion, how can the very youngest children be seen as active social agents within day nurseries and other early years settings?
- Does Roberts' ABC model of well-being provide a useful basis for planning care and education for babies and toddlers? Why? Why not?
- What strategies can be employed to facilitate positive relationships to create an effective 'triangle' for the care of the child?

References

Belenky, M. F., Clinchy, B. M., Goldberger, N. R. and Tarule, J. M. 1997. *Women's Ways of Knowing* (10th Anniversary Edition). New York: Basic Books.

Brooker, L. 2009. 'Just like having a best friend': how babies and toddlers construct relationships with their key workers in nurseries, in T. Papatheodorou and J. Moyles (eds). *Learning Together in the Early Years: Relational Pedagogy*. London: Routledge.

Bruner, J. 1972. The nature and uses of immaturity. *American Psychologist*, 27 (8): 1–22.

Dahlberg, G. and Moss, P. 2005. *Ethics and Politics in Early Childhood Education*. Abingdon: Routledge Falmer.

DfE (Department for Education). 2012. Statutory Framework for the Early Years Foundation Stage. [Online]. Available at https://www.education.gov.uk/publications/standard/AllPublications/Page1/DFE-00023-2012. Accessed January 5, 2013.

Edwards, C. 2012. Teacher and learner, partner and guide: the role of the teacher, in C. Edwards, L. Gandini and G. Forman (eds). *The Hundred Languages of Children: The Reggio Experience in Transformation* (3rd edn). Santa Barbara, CA: Praeger.

Elfer, P. 2005. Observation matters, in L. Abbott and A. Langston (eds). *Birth to Three Matters*. Maidenhead: Open University Press.

Elfer, P., Goldschmied, E. and Selleck, D. 2012. *Key Persons in the Early Years* (2nd edn). London: David Fulton.

Forman, G. and Fyfe, B. 2012. Negotiated learning through design, documentation and discourse, in C. Edwards, L. Gandini and G. Forman (eds). *The Hundred Languages of Children: The Reggio Experience in Transformation* (3rd edn). Santa Barbara, CA: Praeger.

Gerber, M. 2002. *Caring For Infants with Respect*. Expanded edition. Los Angeles, CA: Resources for Infant Educarers (RIE).

Gerhardt, S. 2004. *Why Love Matters: How Affection Shapes a Baby's Brain*. Hove: Brunner-Routledge.

Gopnik, A., Meltzoff, A. and Kuhl, P. 2001. *How Babies Think*. London: Phoenix.

Hohmann, U. 2007. Rights, expertise and negotiations in care and education. *Early Years*, 27 (1): 33–46.

Kaga, Y., Bennett, J. and Moss, P. 2010. *Caring and Learning Together*. Paris: UNESCO.

Katz, L. 1996. Child development knowledge and teacher preparation: confronting assumptions. *Early Childhood Research Quarterly*, 11 (2): 135–146.

Katz, L. G. and Katz, S. J. 2009. *Intellectual Emergencies: Some Reflections on Mothering and Teaching*. Lewisville, NC: Kpress.

Kernan, M. and Singer, E. 2011. *Peer Relationships in Early Childhood Education and Care*. Abingdon: Routledge.

Luff, P. 2009. Responsive work with babies in an English day nursery, in D. Berthelsen, J. Brownlee and E. Johansson (eds). *Participatory Learning in the Early Years: Research and Pedagogy*. London: Routledge.

Martin, E. 2010. Play as an emotional process, in J. Moyles (ed.). *Thinking about Play: Developing a Reflective Approach*. Berkshire: Open University Press.

Martin, E. 2013. Emotional development and learning in early childhood: a qualitative study considering a pedagogy of emotion. Unpublished PhD Thesis. University of Kent, Canterbury.

Montessori, M. 1912. The Montessori Method (translated by A. E. George). New York: Frederick A. Stokes Company. [Online]. Available at http://web.archive.org/web/20050207205651/www.moteaco.com/method/method.html. Accessed April 4, 2012.

Noddings, N. 2003. *Caring: A Feminine Approach to Ethics and Moral Education* (2nd edn). London: University of California Press.

Noddings, N. 2005. Caring in education: the encyclopaedia of informal education. [Online] Available at www.infed.org/biblio/noddings_caring_in_education.htm. Accessed April 4, 2012.

Parker-Rees, R. 2007. Liking to be liked: imitation, familiarity and pedagogy in the first years of life. *Early Years*, 27 (1): 3–17.

Penn, H. 1997. *Comparing Nurseries*. London: Paul Chapman.

Penn, H. 2008. *Understanding Early Childhood: Issues and Controversies* (2nd edn). Maidenhead: McGraw-Hill/Open University Press.

Roberts, R. 2010. *Wellbeing from Birth*. London: Sage Publications.

Rutter, M. 1972. *Maternal Deprivation Reassessed*. Oxford, England: Penguin.

Trevarthen, C. 2002. Learning in companionship: education in the north. *The Journal of Scottish Education*, New series 10 (session 2002–2003): 16–25.

Trevarthen, C. 2003. Infant psychology is an evolving culture. *Human Development*, 46: 233–246.

Trevarthen, C. 2004. Learning about ourselves, from children: why a growing human brain needs interesting companions. University of Edinburgh: Perception-in-action.

[Online]. Available at http://www.perception-in-action.ed.ac.uk/PDFs/Colwyn2004.pdf. Accessed November 16, 2012.

UN Committee on the Rights of the Child. 2005. General Comment 7: Implementing Child Rights in Early Childhood. [Online]. Available at http://www2.ohchr.org/english/bodies/crc/docs/AdvanceVersions/GeneralComment7Rev1.pdf. Accessed February 10, 2012.

Terminology explained

Attachment: The term used by John Bowlby and his colleague Mary Ainsworth to describe the close emotional bond formed between a human infant and his or her main caregiver (usually but not always the birth mother). The attachment bond means that the baby will seek closeness to the adult for protection, desire contact with that person, and experience distress and anxiety when separated.

Companionship: Colwyn Trevarthen described human babies as actively seeking other people and desiring to belong to and participate in communities. Attachments are significant but relationships with babies are also playful and involve communication from an early age.

Developmental psychologists: People who study the growth of human beings and conduct research into the changes that occur in infancy, childhood and throughout the life-span.

Ethics of care: Can be defined as a way of looking at human morality that places attentiveness, responsibility and responsiveness to others at the centre. In contrast to a view of ethics that relies solely on justice and universal rules or laws, an ethics of care describes decisions about right and wrong based upon safeguarding and promoting the interests of the people involved, with particular consideration for those who are most vulnerable. Goodness is therefore judged by the quality of human relationships and well-being.

Social interaction: Describes intentional connection and verbal or non-verbal communication between two or more people (of any age) who are aware of and interested in one another.

CHAPTER

6 Challenges to participatory approaches in early years practice

Jane Gibbs and Linda Cooper

Aims of the chapter

1. To discuss the challenges of delivering the Early Years Foundation Stage (DfE, 2012) whilst maintaining participatory approaches.
2. To celebrate participatory differences in curriculum approaches to working in the early years.
3. To recognise how children can achieve empowerment when they are listened to and heard through their preferred voice.

Introduction

> Children can offer a unique insight into their own learning rather than the practitioner's intention for their learning.
>
> (Pre-school Learning Alliance, 2011: 81)

This chapter explores practical approaches that empower children to become individual agents of their own learning. Whilst it is acknowledged that skilful early years practitioners co-construct the learning process (David, 2001), settings including Montessori schools have long held the belief that children are the masters of their own learning. We also recognise that the Early Years Foundation Stage (EYFS) addresses the need for children to engage in both child-initiated and adult-led play-based activities (DfE, 2012), using exemplars of reflexivity in practice to support sustained shared thinking (Sylva et al., 2006). We will examine the participatory approaches to children's learning in two exemplary early years settings, both having achieved Ofsted outstanding judgements and who acknowledge the individual voices of children and the use of play as a necessary pedagogic tool for young children prior to the more formal didactic junior school years (Goouch, 2009). Bae's (2009) recognition of whether children's choice is considered or controlled by adults will be discussed and a practical approach will be provided in an effort to promote consideration towards children's participation within the early years environment.

Documentary evidence is used from two thriving early years settings and from two different viewpoints. Jane's findings relate to her day-to-day experiences as an Early Years Professional (EYP) and setting leader at Richmond Pre-school, a successful Community Interest Company in Benfleet, Essex. Linda is a PhD scholar and a social researcher who has previously carried out a research project within Absolute Angels, a Montessori pre-school in Coggeshall, Essex. Although both sets of data that we will refer to were originally independently collected for different projects, the joint findings showed that the practitioner and researcher perspectives were identical in exemplifying high quality, child-led activities within the pre-school years. The research projects were undertaken with consent from the university following an ethics application and with full consideration for the children and staff in both settings.

Despite its claim that the EYFS supports playful learning, this can seem contradictory when analysing its numerous developmental matters to be met by each child, the recording of which brings large volumes of administration for the practitioner. Paperwork could be perceived as a hindrance to the quantity of time actually spent in engaging with the children (Luff, 2009).

Best practice at both pre-schools involves not only talking about the need to involve children in decision-making processes, but children's active involvement in settings where children are considered autonomous social agents who participate in constructing their own learning, with adult supporters. This extends to the unlimited time that children have to spend on their chosen activity, which can unintentionally be hindered by practitioners who consider the EYFS as a prescriptive curriculum. In particular children's learning boundaries and expectations (DfE, 2012) could be considered as a further barrier to children's participation, if the practitioners consider themselves to have jurisdiction over the child. Jane will provide a vignette from observations taken within practice and demonstrate how 'A Spiral of Empowerment' (introduced in Chapter 3) could be used, which is an effective tool in encouraging children to feel able to continue as active participants within educational environments.

Linda will provide findings from her research to consider how the Montessori approach supports children to be understood as individuals and participate fully in their own learning, demonstrating how the child-led ethos of Montessori teaching has influenced mainstream early years settings to increase child participation. From the data collected, an argument is made that children who have time and space to create their own playful learning still engage in literacy and numeracy activities, often for longer time periods than potentially prescriptive timetables carried out within school environments. Further, this individual agency is achieved through choice of absorbed play and gives children empowerment in their learning. It also allows practitioners time to observe the children in their care and build on existing knowledge to support further possibilities for learning (Luff, 2009).

Empowering children by listening to their preferred voices

Children express themselves through gestures, actions, sounds, speech and gaze (Flewitt, 2005), which are recognised as 'many languages' within the Reggio Emilia approach (Edwards et al., 1998). Younger children tend to use non-linguistic communication to convey meaning (Reunamo and Nurmilaakso, 2007), which include facial expression, touch, gaze and eye contact (Donaldson, 1995). Flewitt (2005) argues children of *any age or ability* entering an unknown environment could be less likely to use speech as a form of expression, reminding us that not all children are natural talkers. Silin (2006) recognises that even the most talkative children will require periods of time in which they can internalise what happens; therefore their silences should be respected and valued, irrespective of their usual style of communication. Children need to establish rules and protocols within their environment, through observations of their peers and displays of attitudes and behaviours carried out by all stakeholders that they see, which can happen before feeling confident enough to demonstrate their vocal abilities (Flewitt, 2005). Some children appear to be more confident than others and verbalise their needs and desires on entry to the early years environment. Mazzei and Jackson (2012) explain that whatever people/children do or say, we need to consider them and what they see and hear as relative to how they are and how they behave; therefore early years professionals should adopt a sensitive approach that acknowledges and accepts *all* children's preferred forms of expression (DCSF, 2008b), whatever their age or level of confidence.

Participation is generally expressed by children through their involvement in playful activities; however, caution is necessary as some children prefer solitary play in order to assess and gauge what is happening around them. Children's involvement is not always overtly apparent, as '*solitary play*' can indicate the child is disassociated from their environment (Parten, 1932: 249), but Silin (2006) would argue that solitude is a necessity in order for children to internalise occurrences that happen within their environment. Likewise, Franks and Jewitt (2001, cited in Flewitt, 2005: 208) suggest that children's silence may enable them to widen their knowledge of gestures and speech, discovering potential new meanings. Flewitt (2005) has identified that gestures are often used to gain access to play with others after a period of silence, and indicates that children can gauge potential responses through their observations. When children are provided with 'time and space' they can begin to recognise if 'their audience' is influenced by them, which should enable future participation (Lundy, 2007); therefore children's silences are essential within the participatory process, as well as their vocal participation.

We should be able to recognise, through observation, plan the way forward and acknowledge children's contributions based on their preferences for that particular time in their development (DCSF, 2008a). By recognising the child's preferred language of communication, we can provide a '*common ground*' in order to enable '*shared thinking*' (Rogoff et al., 1993: 8). Below is an example of 'best practice' (Box 6.1) which demonstrates the benefit to children if they

BOX 6.1: CASE STUDY EXAMPLE

'Child A' is a girl who has been attending provision for over a year. She attends four three-hour sessions per week. She is very vocal in her communication style and generally happy in nature. She often joins in play with both girls and boys and is quite active. She talks regularly about her home environment and talks through most activities as she participates in them.

I recognise that 'Child A' has begun to change whenever she participates in the gluing activity (as detailed in the observation below). She remains her usual self at all other activities. We provide white PVA glue in pots with paint brush style 'sticks'. Observations are taken over a two-week period, which consist of the following information:

> At the 'glue table' Child A finds a seat furthest away from the other children; if any items come close to her picture she puts her arm around the paper to stop it from going onto the page. She does not converse with any other children who attempted many times to engage in conversation with her and she seems agitated by the attempts of communication. She is spending on average 10–15 minutes per time (activity) drizzling glue from the stick to the page. She positions her head very low and remains focused on the glue, occasionally lifting her head to look at the paper, moving her glue stick over the page while the glue continues to drizzle down. She looks at the picture for a moment when deciding whether it is complete or not and if necessary will continue to drizzle glue across areas of the page. When complete she takes it to the dry rack and goes on to choose another activity, although throughout each session she re-visits it to look at the page and move other children's work away from it.

Analysis of the above information enabled the following extension of learning to take place. *I should be recognised as P (practitioner) and the child as A (as above).*

> P sits down at the glue table prior to A coming over to it. P carries out all the observed behaviours seen by Child A previously (detailed in the summative observations above). Over several sessions A observes P momentarily and after a week A comes and sits next to P; after several moments of silence, A initiates a dialogue with P: 'Are you still doing a wee picture?' P said, 'Yes, are you?' This is the beginning of establishing that A has been watching the glue fall slowly and she tells me that wee falls quickly. She has realised that when the white glue dries it turns 'transparent' which is a new word I introduce to her. She knows she can see through it and it resembles a wet puddle. After our lengthy conversation I ask if she would like to see how quickly water will fall next to glue to see the difference. She is very excited by this and becomes fascinated with the water play as a result. We complete various activities to extend A's thinking; she contributes to many new activities including mixing glue and water and painting shoe boxes with glue and water mix. She even helps me to make playdough which quickly becomes a regular activity with all the children. A was interested in the oil that we added to the flour and the feel of it as she mixed it together.

are provided with a sensitive approach to their silences. Careful thought is given to how the child could be encouraged to share their thoughts and ideas, through the process of analysing the observation and providing a sensitive approach in order to encourage further participation.

Box 6.1 demonstrates how early years practitioners need to observe children carefully over time, to enable them to internalise information and develop at their own pace. Observations are an essential element in the process of getting to know the children, and provide us with invaluable information that enables us to monitor their learning and development (DfE, 2012), while aiding us to plan and develop our approaches to suit them throughout their education within early years provision.

Lundy (2007) recognised that when children are provided with *time and space* they can begin to recognise if they influence 'their audience', which in turn should enable future participation. The example (above) details that Child A initiated communication when she felt ready to, acknowledging that she required the space and time provided, in order to process her thoughts. When communication began on the child's terms P was able to show an interest in what Child A had been thinking and Child A had told P what she would like to do next. Child A was willing to share her views, help to plan and participate further. Developing an ethos of *partnership* with every child is recognised as essential in enabling them to feel they can communicate with us (DfES, 2001). Although the DCSF (2008b) recognises the majority of learning both in pre-school years and beyond is presented verbally, we are reminded that practitioners need to be sensitive to the child's preference of communication in order to provide an inclusive environment where learning can be accessed (DCSF, 2008b).

The mirroring of actions in relation to the example provided above resulted in an empowering experience for the child, which has been summarised in the 'Spiral of Empowerment' (Figure 6.1).

The way Richmond Pre-school approach 'guided participation' varies between circumstances and children; this approach will alter over time as children develop, learn and alter their preferences for communication and learning styles. Staff need to acknowledge children and their beliefs to ensure they feel empowered enough to believe that they can make a difference and that they can play an active role in changing situations within their immediate environment and wider society (Essex County Council, 2010). In Box 6.1, P recognised Child A seemed agitated when others tried to initiate communications with her. Her silence and body language were regarded as essential towards her learning and she was provided with the time and space necessary in which to develop her thoughts (Silin, 2006). To encourage communication in a way that suited her it was necessary to mirror her actions, enabling her to believe that we were sharing thoughts through the process of our actions. Our communications provided a connection between the unknown and the new, which Rogoff et al. (1993)

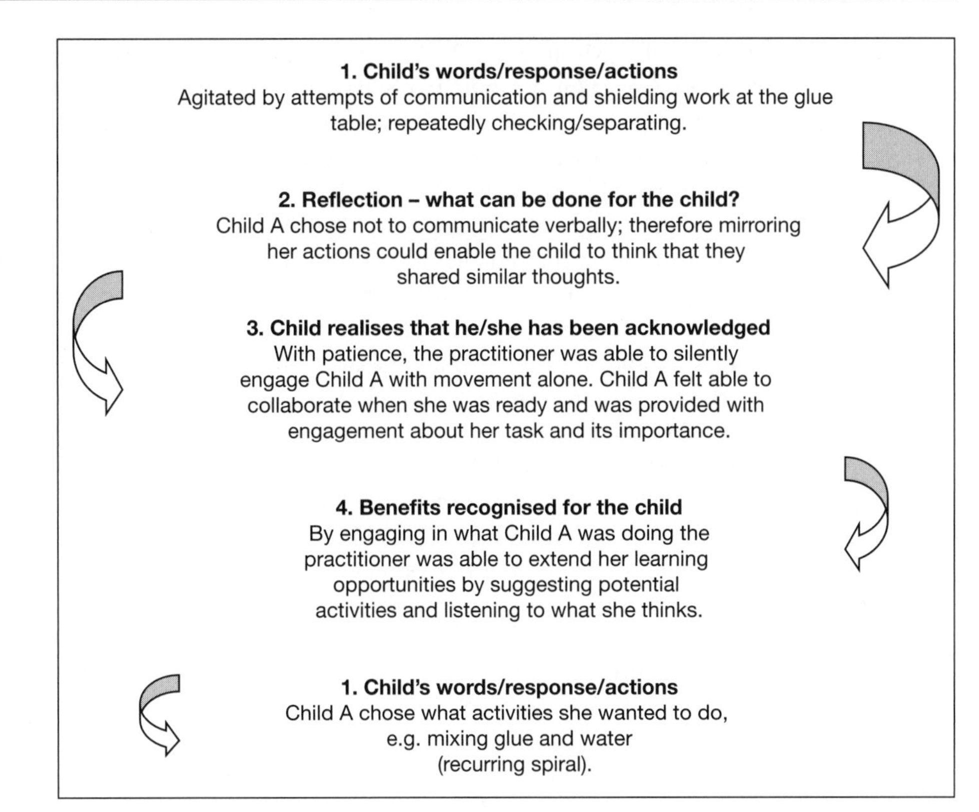

FIGURE 6.1 A Spiral of Empowerment, created by Jane Gibbs and applied to Box 6.1

would recognise as *guided participation*. The 'Spiral of Empowerment' continued for Child A, who appeared empowered and enthused; she regularly shared ideas and knowledge in the realisation that she was understood, listened to and could influence what took place within her environment.

The section below will offer further insight into how an alternative pedagogy (different from Richmond Pre-school) is used in Absolute Angels, a Montessori setting, where child-centred participation is also encouraged within everyday practice, exploring a different but equally insightful case study.

Exploring the Montessori philosophy and principles of the participatory child

Within Montessori settings, children's autonomous decision making is instrumental in the learning process. Children's empowerment, through personal choice of activity and absorbed learning in an enriched pedagogic environment, is a key feature of the Montessori method (Montessori, 1966). The Montessorian approach develops children's knowledge of the world through 'real life' experiences and the practitioner's understanding that children need time to perfect their competencies and skills (Montessori, 2009). Building on Piagetian theory that intellectual development is most productive when children engage in activity as lone learners and are given open ended time to develop their learning, the participatory approach devised by Montessori advocates that children should have free choice and control of their environment and decisions (Stoll Lillard, 2007). The Montessori method explicitly changed early childhood provision by creating child-centred environments that enable children to develop their interests and activities over longer time periods (Mooney, 2000). Allowing children to explore their surroundings and assimilate socio-cultural manners and practices is an explicit learning outcome of Montessorian practice. This makes Montessori pre-schools one of the few learning spaces in which young children actively explore their learning environment within a lone or group context, whilst becoming socially adept with their peers (Stoll Lillard, 2007).

The philosophy and methodology that underpin Montessori teaching is that children are masters of their own learning. This involves giving children time and space to explore their own surroundings and learn at their own pace (Montessori, 2009). It is recognised, however, that giving children this amount of freedom is often seen by other educational settings as a challenge to the expertise of the practitioner. In this respect, practitioners in other settings can be seen as showing tokenism towards participation (Hart, 1997) rather than empowering children to make choices and express ideas and opinions for themselves. Mazzei and Jackson (2012) highlight the danger of power relations and researchers' own 'agenda' in qualitative research, an important consideration when researching children.

Canning (2007) acknowledges the need for play in the construction of children's development of the self. Allowing children to express themselves through their preferred voice is key to the skill of the Montessori practitioner in scaffolding children's learning. This freedom can oppose regular teaching practice, but can ultimately reap rewards for the child learner (Soundy, 2003). Practitioners in Montessori settings do not instigate or lead the learning process; rather they provide support when requested by the child. This ethos of care, which translates into child-led practice is evident at Absolute Angels, as developmental skills are achieved whilst children remain in full control over their learning choices.

I visited Absolute Angels as a researcher to investigate the application of the EYFS within a Montessori setting. I had no previous working or personal relationship with any of the practitioners, parents or children at Absolute Angels prior to the observations. Of particular interest was the exploration of the quality of literacy provision and how it is achieved within a holistic learning environment, where attention is given to physical, emotional and intellectual needs to promote language, literacy and motor development (Montessori, 2009).

In line with common themes of Montessorian settings, Absolute Angels is a large open plan, naturally lit building, with natural coloured equipment and toys. The layout of the setting is considered a further way to engage cognitive learning, as children negotiate their spatial awareness between play sections (Stoll Lillard, 2007). The equipment on offer to the children is often 'real life', such as cooking utensils. The wall mounted displays are all at children's eye level, including the clock. No primary colours are used and in this way the holistic feel of the environment is kept, without 'sensory overload'. All activities are children driven and practitioners offer choices for the children in which to participate, but it is the children's choice whether they wish to engage.

There were two major differences between other mainstream settings and Absolute Angels that Linda witnessed during her observations. First was the quiet and orderly fashion in which the children engaged with their playing and interaction with each other. The practitioners come down to the children's eye level when speaking with them, rather than speaking 'down at them'. The second difference was the length of time children remained immersed in their chosen activity. Observations at other settings had seen children darting from one activity to another constantly. At Absolute Angels, continuous absorbed play is commonplace. Absolute Angels' principal, Sarah Rowledge, also runs one of 120 accredited Montessori nurseries and primary schools overseen by Ofsted and Montessori. Sarah is a highly respected Montessorian; she is National Chair for Primary Montessori and on the Montessori Evaluation and Accreditation Board (MEAB), Essex. Further, being Deputy Chair for the Region, she witnesses the importance of acquiring concentration as a skill to take forward in the transition to formal primary education, in order for a child to manage the more prescriptive demands of the National Curriculum. Vignette 6.1 demonstrates explicitly an example of children immersed in absorbed, child-led learning.

VIGNETTE 6.1

Several examples were observed that displayed unusually long periods of children concentrating on their activity. For one of the sessions, three boys sat and read independently and continuously for an hour and a quarter.

Vignette 6.1 is an example of how the Montessori setting can deconstruct the stereotypical view of boys having a deficit attention span and support academic learning that is child led (Stoll Lillard, 2007). Children having the ability to be immersed in an activity is hindered in some settings by the pressure on practitioners to fulfil EYFS criteria or for the children to be productive and to have something 'to show' for their time in the session, although a simple photograph can provide an insight into the high levels of concentration that children possess. Long before the implementation of the EYFS, Montessori herself (1966: 183) described this 'conflict between adult and child' in different interpretations of each other's 'work'. Absolute Angels still have to achieve the developmental matters of the EYFS, but skilful monitoring by the staff means they observe the children undertaking a particular learning outcome and they are able to record this as part of the children's learning journeys.

VIGNETTE 6.2

A misconception of Montessori pre-schools is that children do not voluntarily choose to engage in literacy activities.

The literacy corner in Absolute Angels was explored and played in by many of the children choosing to read, write, trace letters in the sandbox, colour, paint and play with words and letters in grammar boxes, using equipment common in Montessori settings (Stoll Lillard, 2007). Further, children also asked practitioners to read to them or initiate circle time with action songs to explore other literacy skills. Books were fully available to read and to take home after the sessions. It could be interpreted that children who are not approaching the literacy area of their own choosing are not ready for formal schooling. Practitioners respect children's decisions whether or not to engage in more academic activities within the setting, as they recognise that teaching literacy at a young age may be counterproductive and discourage children from prescriptive learning in later school years (Alexander, 2009).

The practitioners at Absolute Angels invited Linda to share her findings after initial observations, which demonstrated their wish to share reciprocal and progressive skills, showing reflexivity in their practice to support sustained shared thinking (Sylva et al., 2006). This helps to co-construct knowledge and to improve the learning environment available to their children (Moss, 2006). The practitioners at Absolute Angels are showing their willingness to be co-researchers in their children's learning. Montessori teaching considers the learning of literacy skills as a personal learning journey, which should evolve when the child is interested and willing to learn (Montessori, 1966). There are challenges, however, as there is the necessity to fulfil EYFS compliance and produce evidence of learning outcomes, which is at odds with the Montessori ethos. As such the setting needs to conform to EYFS whilst maintaining its ideals of child-led learning. Montessori schools have historically based their ongoing assessment of their children on observations to progress their children's learning (Montessori, 1966), but now have to include written and photographic evidence to meet EYFS developmental matters. These are everyday challenges faced by practitioners in all early years settings. The vignettes used here support the argument that alternative approaches such as the Montessori method can be used in collaboration with EYFS guidelines, to enable the child to become the master of his own environment (Montessori, 2009).

The notion of children being in complete control of every session could be a further challenge to some mainstream practitioners who are used to leading and directing all activities. Absolute Angels exhibit an invisible pedagogy (Bernstein, 1999), where experience and contribution create learning opportunities both by the children and with co-construction by the practitioners, to work harmoniously for the benefit of the children's progress. Curriculum need and individual outcomes can be considered in terms of horizontal and vertical discourses (Bernstein, 1999) that consider how learning outcomes and prescriptive, educational milestones can be achieved whilst meeting the unique needs of each child. Absolute Angels achieves this by both adhering to EYFS guidelines and allowing free flow play to exist.

VIGNETTE 6.3

Three girls came to the literacy corner. They copied each other – one came to take her name off the board and trace around and two others followed. They put the equipment away when they were finished. Three more girls engaged in colouring and put their 'work' in their name trays to take home. Another girl played with letters on a magnetic board.

Vignette 6.3 highlights the children's voluntary engagement with literacy play, whilst following the Montessori way of tidying away after each activity. A practitioner was in the immediate vicinity for support if needed, but she did not interact in this instance.

Enabling children to act as social agents is an important aspect of inclusive, participatory practice (Hart, 1997) as their insight could influence change for children on an individual level through inclusion in the decision-making process, or at an institutional level through the practitioner's reflective practice. Ultimately, children's opinions could make a positive, strategic contribution, which supports the community and environment, as outlined in the five outcomes of Every Child Matters (DfES, 2004). The participatory approach at Absolute Angels encourages independent, free-thinking children capable of individual learning. This reinforces dialogic pedagogy through the example in Vignette 6.3 above, highlighting the learning experience as a reflexive one between adult and child and the importance of listening to all children's voices (Soundy, 2003). Clark and Statham (2005) share their belief that children are experts in their own lives and that working alongside them strengthens their identity and control. To Linda, who is a social researcher and a mother of two, this aspirational ideal of expression and uniqueness in each child is one to be celebrated.

Summary and conclusion

Both Absolute Angels and Richmond Pre-school apply different interpretations of pedagogy, yet allow their children's voices to be heard in order that children are empowered in their own learning. Their styles may be different, but both strive to deliver their version of what is best for the children and thus consider their individual notions of the purest form of participatory learning in the process whilst ensuring the children remain inspired and empowered throughout practice.

Points to consider and questions to ask yourself

- How do you ensure that you listen to children's preferred voices and act upon them effectively?
- What strategies can be used to encourage activities in early years settings that are as child led as possible?

Acknowledgements

Grateful thanks is given to Sarah Rowledge for her support and agreement for Absolute Angels to be included in this chapter and to her team for their co-operation and assistance during Linda's observation periods.

Thank you to all the staff at Richmond Pre-school who always support and encourage Jane's endless alterations to provision, in order that we provide what we consider to be the best outcomes for all children who attend.

References

Alexander, R. (ed.). 2009. *Children, Their World, Their Education: Final Report and Recommendations of the Cambridge Primary Review*. Abingdon: Routledge.

Bae, B. 2009. Children's right to participate – challenges in everyday interactions. *European Early Childhood Education Research Journal*, 17 (3): 391–406.

Bernstein, B. 1999. Vertical and horizontal discourses: an essay. *British Journal of Sociology of Education*, 20 (2): 157–173.

Canning, N. 2007. Children's empowerment in play. *European Early Childhood Education Research Journal*, 15 (2): 227–236.

Clark, A. and Statham, J. 2005. Listening to children: experts in their own lives. *Adoption and fostering*, 29 (1): 45–56.

David, T. 2001. Curriculum in the early years, in G. Pugh (ed.). *Contemporary Issues in the Early Years* (3rd edn). London: Sage.

de Bono, E. 1991. *I Am Right, You Are Wrong*. London: Penguin Books Limited.

DCSF (Department for Children, Schools and Families). 2004. *Every Child Matters: Change for Children*. Nottingham: DCSF.

DCSF (Department for Children, Schools and Families). 2008a. *The Early Years Foundation Stage: Setting the Standards for Learning, Development and Care for Children from Birth to Five*. Nottingham: DCSF.

DCSF (Department for Children, Schools and Families). 2008b. *Working Together: Listening to the Voices of Children and Young People*. Nottingham: DCSF.

DCSF (Department for Children, Schools and Families). 2010. *Inclusion Development Programme: Supporting Children with Behavioural, Emotional and Social Difficulties: Guidance for Practitioners in the Early Years Foundation Stage*. Nottingham: DCSF.

DfE (Department for Education). 2012. *The Early Years Foundation Stage*. Cheshire: DfE.

DfES (Department for Education and Skills). 2001. *SEN Toolkit. Section 4: Enabling Pupil Participation*. Nottingham: DfES.

DfES (Department for Education and Skills). 2004. *Every Child Matters: Change for Children*. Nottingham: DfES.

Donaldson, M. L. 1995. *Children with Language Impairments: An Introduction*. London: Jessica Kingsley Publishers.

Edwards, C., Gandini, L. and Forman, C. (eds). 1998. *The Hundred Languages of Children*. Norwood, NJ: Ablex.

Essex County Council. 2010. *I Know I Matter to You*. Chelmsford: Essex County Council.

Flewitt, R. 2005. Is every child's voice heard? Researching the different ways 3-year-old children communicate and make meaning at home and in a pre-school playgroup. *Early Years*, 25 (3): 207–222.

Goouch, K. 2009. Forging and fostering relationships in play: whose zone is it anyway? in T. Papatheodorou and J. Moyles (eds). *Learning Together in the Early Years: Exploring Relational Pedagogy*. London: Routledge.

Hart, R. A. 1997. *Children's Participation: The Theory and Practice of Involving Young Citizens in Community Development and Environmental Care*. London: Earthscan.

Luff, P. 2009. Looking, learning, listening and linking: uses of observation for relational pedagogy, in T. Papatheodorou and J. Moyles (eds). *Learning Together in the Early Years: Exploring Relational Pedagogy*. London: Routledge.

Lundy, L. 2007. Voice is not enough: conceptualising Article 12 of the United Nations Convention on the Rights of the Child. *British Educational Research Journal*, 33 (6): 927–942.

Maslow, A. 1970. *Motivation and Personality*. New York: Harper and Row.

Mazzei, L. A. and Jackson, A. Y. 2012. Complicating voice in a refusal to 'let participants speak for themselves'. *Qualitative Inquiry*, 18 (9): 745–758.

Montessori, M. 1966. *The Secret of Childhood*. New York: Ballantine Books.

Montessori, M. 2009. *The Absorbent Mind* (9th edn). Miami, FL: BN Publishing.

Mooney, C. G. 2000. *Theories of Childhood*. St. Paul, MN: Redleaf Press.

Moss, P. 2006. Structures, understandings and discourses: possibilities for the early childhood worker. *Contemporary Issues in Early Childhood*, 7 (1): 30–41.

Parten, M. B. 1932. Social participation among pre-school children. [Online]. *Journal of Abnormal and Social Psychology*, 24: 243–269. Accessed March 1, 2011.

Pound, L. 2005. *How Children Learn*. London: Step Forward Publishing.

Pre-school Learning Alliance. 2011. The new child in focus – sample pages. [Online]. Available at www.pre-school.org.uk/document/562. Accessed November 4, 2011.

Reunamo, J. and Nurmilaakso, M. 2007. Vygotsky and agency in language development. *European Early Childhood Education Research Journal*, 15 (3): 313–327.

Rogoff, B., Mistry, J., Göncü, A. and Mosier, C. 1993. Guided Participation in Cultural Activity by Toddlers and Caregivers. *Monographs of the Society for Research in Child Development*. Serial no. 236, 58 (8): 1–179.

Senge, P. M. 2006. *The Fifth Discipline: The Art and Practice of the Learning Organisation*. London: Random House.

Silin, J. G. 2006. Who can speak? Silence, voice and pedagogy, in N. Yelland (ed.). *Critical Issues in Early Childhood Education*. Berkshire: Open University Press.

Soundy, C. S. 2003. Portraits of exemplary Montessori practice for all literacy teachers. *Early Childhood Education Journal*, 31 (2): 127–131.

Stoll Lillard, A. 2007. *Montessori: The Science behind the Genius* (2nd edn). Oxford: Oxford University Press.

Sylva, K., Siraj-Blatchford, I., Taggart, B., Sammons, P., Melhuish, E., Elliot, K. and Totsika, V. 2006. Capturing quality in early childhood through environmental rating scales. *Early Childhood Research Quarterly*, 21 (1): 76–92.

Terminology explained

Common ground: Providing inclusive practice by adapting what we do/have in order to meet all children's preferences/needs.

Developmental matters: The development milestones expected to be demonstrated within the age bands specified within the Early Years Foundation Stage.

Horizontal and vertical discourses: The interconnection of two different ways of looking at the same issue.

Invisible pedagogy: Hidden or underlying methods and theories of teaching.

Reflexivity: Making an immediate reflection and acting on it straightaway; otherwise known as reflecting-in-action.

Solitary play: When a child appears to prefer their own company throughout an activity.

Sustained shared thinking: To enable recognition that we are sharing similar thoughts and ideas, can understand and continue with these.

PART

Children's participation and research

CHAPTER

7 Participatory approaches in research involving children

Mallika Kanyal, Paulette Luff, Linda Cooper and Rebecca Webster

Aims of the chapter

1. To explore the meaning of 'participation' from a research perspective, considering its origin from the broader area of participatory research.
2. To discuss the role participatory approaches can play in promoting children's rights.
3. To share the use of various participatory methods and techniques in researches involving children.

Introduction

The chapter aims to discuss the role of participatory research in promoting children's rights. Various methods and techniques used in participatory research are discussed, with an emphasis on their use within education settings. A detailed description of each method within the context of empirical research is outside the scope of this chapter, but references are made to the concept of participatory research, its origin, philosophical claims, ethics and critique, with an aim to help the reader understand the conceptual background behind any participatory work. The methods described here are mainly derived from the authors' personal research work, with each work divided into different sections, discussing a method of enquiry and/or its use within an education and care setting.

Section 1 is a general introduction to participatory approaches to research, with a focus on participatory research (PR). Section 2 describes drawings as a participatory method, with examples taken from an exploratory research work undertaken by the author with young children in a primary school in England and India. Section 3 refers to interviews as a medium to help children talk about their experiences, again in an education context. The example is taken from the same exploratory study, with emphasis placed on children's voice. Section 4 gives a general account of the use of questionnaires as a research method, taking examples from secondary researches. Section 5 refers to the use of visual and aural technology as tools to enhance children's participation in research. Here the author has taken examples from her research of using video cameras with young children. Section 6 gives an account of observation as a strategy for participation. The author acknowledges the participatory nature of observations as recognised by pioneers as well as contemporary theorists.

SECTION 1
INTRODUCTION TO PARTICIPATORY APPROACHES IN RESEARCH

Mallika Kanyal

The use and benefit of participatory approaches has been echoed by various authors and researchers in a range of education contexts. Clark, McQuail and Moss (2003), and Clark and Moss (2006), for example, use participatory approaches to listen to the 'voice of the child' and introduce the Mosaic approach within education. The Mosaic approach encourages children's participation not only through 'spoken words' but also by integrating 'visual' with 'verbal'. They used participatory approaches to the extent where children participated and expressed their views and ideas in designing new learning environments for themselves (see Clark, 2010). Kellett (2010) similarly has been working successfully with children and young people and empowering them as active researchers. Her work at the Children's Research Centre (The Open University, UK) promotes children and young people's voice by training and supporting them to investigate issues they identify as important to them.

The use of these approaches, whether in practice or research, has been recognised to promote children's right to participation as they encourage the child to take an active part in various processes, acknowledging them as equal partners. Considering this from a practice perspective, children's partnership in educational processes is believed to be providing a more responsive and sustainable pedagogical environment, thereby enhancing children's learning experiences (Pascal and Bertram, 2009). Whilst understanding these approaches from a research perspective, it can be said to be enabling children to value their own knowledge and develop a capacity to participate rationally (Pant, n.d.). These processes, however, must be meaningful for both the children and adults, and provide opportunities where both groups can share their views and perspectives in a mutual, shared and democratic environment. This is particularly important in an education context which is traditionally associated with power imbalances between the teacher and children.

History of participatory approaches

Reverting to the history of participatory approaches, their origin has generally been linked with the empowerment of the disadvantaged, studied under the umbrella of participatory research (PR). The main aim of participatory research has been to empower the marginalised, taking a human activist approach, thereby giving it an explicit political agenda (Gouin et al., 2011). The origin of participatory research can be argued to have developed from two (inter-related) traditions: (a) the action research school developed by the social psychologist Kurt Lewin in the 1940s; and (b) the (social) work with oppressed communities in South America, Asia, and Africa in the 1970s (Minkler, 2004). Kurt Lewin's work on action research gives PR an emphasis on the action–reflection cycle by the participants in order to take action to bring about change (Minkler, 2004), in a collaborative environment (Gouin et al., 2011). The work with oppressed communities can especially be linked to the work of Paulo Freire, Orlando Fals Borda and Feminist researchers, who worked towards establishing alternative approaches to counter the hegemonic nature of research for knowledge construction (McIntyre, 2008). This enriches the conceptualisation of participatory research as an alternative approach to conventional research (Minkler, 2004; McIntyre, 2008). Participatory research, since then, has been used as an umbrella term for different approaches of participatory inquiry, originating mainly from the criticism of positivist research and a critique of the role of researcher in the less developed world (Riet, 2008). On a general principle, PR can be identified from a partnership approach which seeks to break down the barriers between the researcher and the researched (Minkler, 2004), with an aim to create a democratic and socially 'safe space' for the participants to participate freely within various degrees of participation (Bergold and Thomas, 2012).

Philosophical claims of participatory research

In order to validate the empirical position of participatory research, it is important to explore its philosophical claims. Various authors and researchers, such as Cornwall and Jewkes (1995), Pant (n.d.) and Riet (2008), have argued for PR to be an appropriate approach for the study of human action, especially within the domain of social sciences (including Education). The techniques and participatory learning actions within PR make it a valuable process to understand social and human actions, which may be otherwise difficult to study using traditional approaches of enquiry. Participatory research, therefore, can be seen in direct contrast with the positivist paradigm of research which believes in generalisation and universalisation of knowledge through objective methodology (Punch, 2011). For the study of humans, who live in a socially complex world, it may be difficult to give a precise explanation of their behaviours and actions through positivist enquiry methods only (Cohen et al., 2011) and therefore require special attention. This is where participatory approaches play an important role as they have the capacity to move beyond the individual mind and consider the social aspect of reality through studying humans' dialogic interaction (Riet, 2008), strengthening the philosophical position of participatory research. This increases the likelihood of rationalising PR under the anti-positivist paradigm, inclined more towards the qualitative methods of investigation (not ruling out the possibility of quantitative measures). Qualitative approaches are better suited to study complex human behaviour and actions as these experiences are perceived to be situated within everyday working practices of those involved (Wimpenny, 2010), a locale which is considered prime in any participative research. An application of participatory methods and techniques can, however, have various implications on research processes as it mostly involves studying human behaviour in group situations. These may give rise to ethical dilemmas, some of which are discussed below.

Ethics and participatory research with children

A consideration of ethical issues is vital to collect any high quality evidence, not only in researches involving children, but in any research involving human participants. Thomas and O'Kane (1998) point towards the common ethical issues that researchers face in research with any age group. These issues are related to obtaining an informed consent; well-being of participants; confidentiality; and power imbalance between the researcher and those being researched. Thomas and O'Kane (1998) further argue that although important in any research, these issues present more sharply if the research participants are children – partly due to the power imbalances between adults and children, the difference in children's understanding and experience of the world, the different ways children communicate and also due to the complicated nature of gatekeeper and child protection procedures.

In any research involving children, researchers must pay special attention to the power and status imbalances between the adults and children, which Morrow and Richards (1996) regard as the biggest ethical challenge. A lack of engagement with ethical issues can create a significant barrier to high quality evidence (Robert-Holmes, 2005).

In order to overcome this problem, Morrow and Richards (1996) suggest using non-invasive, non-confrontational and participatory methods in research, some of which are discussed later in this chapter. The application of participatory methods, however, does not come without challenges. The biggest challenge is for the adults to move away from their (natural) paternal role of speaking *for* the children. In order to establish an ethical and participatory environment, the paternal role needs to be substituted with that of an enabling one, which makes it possible for the children to speak or act on *behalf of themselves* without being dependent on adults to advocate their voices (Tickle, 1999). An over-protective attitude of adults towards children may therefore reduce children's ability to participate effectively in research processes (Morrow and Richards, 1996).

Grey and Winter (2011) further relate power imbalances to the concept of 'consent' and 'assent'. 'Assent', they argue, is generally associated with children's agreement to participate in research and 'consent' is linked with adults' permission, making the former less important. They therefore favour the use of the term 'consent' with both groups as irrespective of gaining adult permission; it is unethical to carry out research with a reluctant child. However, to enable researchers to gain access to children, it is important to obtain permission from 'gatekeepers', who in an education context may be teachers, social workers, parents and carers. Grey and Winter (2011) acknowledge the important role of the gatekeepers, especially for the children who find it difficult to dissent or disagree, but conversely argue that while protecting the agency of the children and withholding their consent, gatekeepers might further marginalise the underrepresented groups.

Box 7.1 shows examples of obtaining consent from children to participate in research. The two researches mentioned here aimed at exploring the use of participatory approaches in understanding children's perceptions of their school environment (5–6 years old), and nursery environment (3.5–5 years old).

In order to avoid issues related to consent, Thomas and O'Kane (1998) suggest three principles. The first principle involves an active agreement on the part of the child and a passive agreement on the part of the caretaker. The second principle acknowledges and respects children's withdrawal from the study at any point they like, whether it is expressed explicitly in the form of a dissent or through non-verbal cues such as body language (Grey and Winter, 2011). The third principle relates to giving choice to children in how they want to participate in research (consistent with the objectives of the study).

A careful consideration of all these issues within participatory work will not only strengthen research's methodology but also improve its reliability and validity (Thomas and O'Kane, 1998).

Critique of participatory research

Besides the recognised benefits of participatory research, there are certain uncertainties which lie within the use of participatory approaches. One such uncertainty and misconception is in our understanding of the term 'power', usually recognised as an absolute attribute that can be handed over from the researcher to the researched (Holland et al., 2010). Power, instead, is a more relational and contextual concept that needs to be seen in a continuum (Holland et al., 2010). More emphasis needs to be placed on *how* participation is enacted rather than *how* much participation is achieved.

In order to understand how to enact participation, its general application can be explained through various approaches and models that explain the basic theory behind participation (Kellett, 2010), some of which are explained and critiqued in Chapter 4. However, on a precautionary note, no approach can be regarded as inherently participatory as its degree of participation is determined

BOX 7.1: GETTING CHILDREN'S CONSENT TO PARTICIPATE IN RESEARCH

The first research study was aimed at exploring children's perceptions of their school environment (children of 5–6 years old) in a primary school in east England and north India. In order to obtain consent, the research tasks were first explained to the children using easy to comprehend pictures. These pictures were included in the consent form and the children were given one day to think about their participation in the research and also to discuss it with their parents, should they wish to. The aim was to help children make an informed decision about their participation. They were also given information on how to be able to decline their participation and told that this would not affect their class activities in any way.

The next day children were asked to vote their response (their photograph with their name on it) in one of the three boxes: thumbs up face box (for showing their willingness to participate), face with a 'thinking' expression (demonstrating that they cannot decide or need more time to think), or a thumbs down face box (demonstrating that they do not wish to participate). It was anticipated that children would be able to label their pictures, and, if not, as researchers, we were prepared to help the children write their names on them.

All participating children readily gave their consent to participate in research the next day. Had they put their picture in the 'thinking face' (consent) box, they would have had the research procedure explained to them again and given another day to think about their participation. The whole procedure, using the three boxes, would have been repeated.

Likewise, in the second research study, which aimed at exploring children's perceptions of their nursery environment (children of 3.5–5 years old), we used an image-based information booklet to explain research tasks and to record children's consent. This time we used a scrapbook which was read to children in the form of a story, explaining research tasks (with the help of picture cues and also photographs of the research team members) and then their consent was recorded in the form of traffic lights. The consent was recorded each day before children participated in research activities, after explaining the tasks to them. Grey and Winter (2011) believe that giving too much information at the start of a project may confuse young children. The process of obtaining consent every time children engage in research activities may give them multiple opportunities to either give or withhold consent. It is advisable to first practise the consent activities with children (for example, the use of traffic lights) in the form of general routine activities as it helps them understand the process. We practised the traffic light system with children as part of their favourite food activity.

by the way that model/method is used. The true participatory nature of each method is therefore tested 'in action' (Crivello et al., 2009) and not just in theory. It therefore becomes essential to adopt participatory methods and techniques that can help to break down power differentials, often based on age, status, class, gender, ethnicity and other related factors. The assumption that the tools somehow would enable participation is yet problematic. Attention needs to be paid to the details of design and relational aspects of research which potentially can provide enabling conditions for true participation (Waller and Bitou, 2011).

Another major criticism of participatory work is around the issue of representation. Riet (2008) raises concerns about the value of knowledge produced through participatory research and the extent to which it can claim to be a truthful representation of reality. Campbell et al. (2007) argue that a true representation may remain a valid criticism of participatory research (just like other methodologies) as participation can never be forced; it will have to remain voluntary. There also seems to be more emphasis placed on the process of participatory research rather than the impact (Holland et al., 2010).

A further question is whether participatory research is actually a contemporary research method or a form or extension of the long-established traditions of ethnographic research (Gallacher and Gallagher, 2008; Holland et al., 2010). More research needs to be done to explore the similarities and differences in the conceptualisation of these two research approaches.

When considering the application of participatory research in education (early years and beyond), I would argue that participatory approaches have already created a niche in education and their benefits are being realised in a range of contexts, for example see Clark, 2010; Kellett, 2010; Campbell et al., 2007; and Seale, 2010. It can, however, have multiple meanings and interpretations, depending upon the context they are being applied to. Participation, therefore, is regarded as a socially constructed phenomenon, the conceptualisation of which is influenced by our everyday practices, values and behaviours that we as a social group uphold and believe in, which further influences the research approaches that we choose to adopt.

Realising this from a pedagogical research position, it is suggestive to acknowledge the situated nature of children's experiences, because participatory methods may not always represent a generalised social reality. The methods we choose to understand children's perspectives may have institutional or researchers' bias. The research on children's voice and their participation, therefore, should not be regarded as individual, fixed, straightforward, linear or clear, but instead as socially co-constructed (Komulainen, 2007: 18, 23) which can be shaped by multiple factors, such as researchers' own assumptions about children, their particular use of language, the institutional contexts in which researchers operate and the overall ideological climate which prevails (Spyrou, 2011). Listening thereafter should be regarded reflexively to include interpretation, meaning making and responding (Clark et al., 2003), a process which has both transformative and empowering potential.

When considering participatory research from a 'rights' perspective, it recognises children's competent side but can often hide their vulnerable side (Kjørholt, 2005). We therefore need to use participative research methods with a caveat that children may choose to express themselves in a range of ways, be it vocal, an artefact or their silence. Furthermore, in order to create a shared participative research environment, it is paramount to consider participation from both a children's rights as well as responsibility perspective. This involves not only listening to a child's view but also attending to other fellow children's and adults' views, who are integral to the (learning) environment. The argument goes back to the principles of 'connectedness', 'interaction' and 'relationships', the aspects of pedagogy which can be honed by the application of participatory approaches. The impetus for applying participatory research approaches can therefore be drawn from the notions of 'culture of participation' (Kanyal, 2012) and 'guided participation' (Rogoff et al., 1993). Culture of participation acknowledges the inclusiveness which can be realised by including different stakeholders' views, for example including the perspectives of adults as well as peers. There may be challenges associated with this due to power differentials and the level of influence that different stakeholders can have in the running of an institution. It therefore becomes vital to have an interaction and alignment of the values and attitudes of different stakeholders in education to encourage a truly participative environment (Kanyal, 2012). Similarly, Rogoff et al. (1993) suggest that participation can be promoted by actively involving *all* participants within the (learning) communities, which draws on the cultural tools and support from adults and others to jointly problem solve (Rogoff et al., 1993). In a learning community, we therefore cannot limit participative research to include only a child's voice but look wider and include the views of adults and other fellow children within. This can be researched using the 'collective (participatory) methods' which aim to facilitate a group with shared meanings, interests or experiences to analyse or access those experiences (Veale, 2005). Collective methods can, however, hide inequitable participation and may lead to the generation of false consensus (Veale, 2005). The processes can also privilege the already privileged (Bragg, 2007). This especially needs to be considered while researching with bigger participant sizes. More research, therefore, needs to be done to develop more creative methods of attending to collective participation and collective decision making with children.

Considering the criticism cited above, it becomes apparent that in order to get convincing answers to these questions, more evidence needs to be gathered and analysed systematically and that participatory research methods should not be considered uncritically (Waller and Bitou, 2011). A careful consideration of the methodology and appropriate research methods is therefore needed in order to make a research design truly participative.

What do participatory methods entail?

Participatory research includes an adoption of a range of traditional as well as novel methods, primarily influenced by Participatory Rural Appraisal (PRA) techniques used in developing countries contexts (Crivello et al., 2009). PRA mainly involves working with the communities characterised by low levels of literacy, limited experience of interaction with the government or bureaucracy and language barriers. It therefore makes more use of the vivid, graphic and concrete features which have been proven to work efficiently with children (Thomas and O'Kane, 1998: 342). Novel approaches can be activity based and involve visual representation, such as mapping, modelling, diagramming, photography and time lines; and estimation, such as ranking and matrix (Crivello et al., 2009; Riet, 2008). It can also include conventional approaches like semi-structured interviews, case studies and oral histories (Riet, 2008). Inclusion of a range of techniques and approaches demonstrates the belief of participatory approaches that creation of knowledge is not limited to written or spoken words, but includes active representations of ideas, the use of symbols, drawings, and even direct activity in the context of study (Riet, 2008). The use of participatory approaches can therefore assist in breaking down the imbalances of power, not only due to the children having a greater control over the agenda and more time and space to talk about the issues that concern them, but also by creating an atmosphere in which there are no right or wrong answers and even some opportunities for children to interpret and explain their own data (Thomas and O'Kane, 1998: 343).

The section below describes some of the participatory methods that potentially can be used in participatory research and also in practice to encourage children's participation in education and care.

SECTION 2
USING DRAWINGS TO UNDERSTAND CHILDREN'S PERCEPTIONS OF THEIR LEARNING ENVIRONMENT

Mallika Kanyal

Drawings, as evident from the history of participatory research, have been regarded as an important research technique to understand local people's perceptions of their environment. They have the capacity to give participants the freedom and flexibility to express their views without relying solely on the spoken word, a method which is heavily influenced by traditional research methods.

Children's drawings have been used to understand varied perceptions of the world around them. These perceptions have mainly been understood from an adult's perspective rather than the child's explanation of what the drawings are about (Fargas-Malet et al., 2010). Such practices may sustain a tokenistic attitude of adults towards children's participation, which adopts a paternalistic approach to showcase children's experiences on behalf of them. With an emphasis on the use of participatory research in education, more attention is now being paid to what the *children* say about *their* drawings. Various researchers and authors have used children's drawings effectively to illustrate children's perceptions, demonstrating the use of drawings as an effective research tool.

Studies like Anning and Ring (2004) and Weber and Mitchell (1995) illustrate how drawings can be used to help educators and other professionals understand the lives of children in schools and related settings, for example to demonstrate teachers' pedagogic styles and children's achievement in schools (Bonoti et al., 2003). Drawings, in education, can be said to be a 'natural' method of enquiry as children in schools are frequently given opportunities and tools to draw 'for fun' (Walker, 2007: 99). As children spend a majority of their time in schools, schools can therefore be argued to be a part of children's everyday culture, informing their meaning making (Kendrick and McKay, 2004). Children's drawings hence can be argued to be more than a simple representation of what they see before them and can be better understood as the ways in which they are making sense of their experiences (Anning and Ring, 2004). Children also draw with full care and attention when it comes to using them as a tool to illustrate their experience (Hill, 2006). Drawings, therefore, can sufficiently be used as a research method offering insight into children's individual experiences (Veale, 2005).

Fargas-Malet et al. (2010) give a detailed account of the strengths and challenges of using drawings as a research instrument with children. On a positive note, drawings can be used as a good ice-breaker, helping children to relax and establish rapport. It may offer children more control as participants as it gives them an opportunity to draw as much or as little as they like. On a precautionary side, not all children might find drawing an enjoyable activity; older children might see it as 'babyish'. There is also a possibility that children may copy each other's drawing, thus illustrating a socially constructed rather than an individual idea. Another dilemma of children's drawings is the focus on the end product rather than the process itself. The end product of children's drawings, although important, does not always reflect the narrative that they utter whilst engaged in the process. It is therefore vital to record children's simultaneous utterances as they help to weave stories around the mark making. It can potentially communicate the intentions and children's thinking to the researcher (Coates and Coates, 2006).

Below is an example (Box 7.2) where children's drawings are used as participatory tools to enable them to describe their everyday experiences at school.

As evident from the examples, it is clear that children are able to articulate their perceptions through the use of drawings and that the drawings are very much representative of children's cultural contexts. The actual school drawings here show the difference in classroom resources and layout within the schools

BOX 7.2: CHILDREN'S DRAWINGS

The example described here is part of an exploratory study which aimed at understanding children's perceptions of their learning environment. Children aged 5–6 years (class 1) from a primary school in east England and north India participated in the study using multiple participatory approaches, amongst which drawings were one of the methods (for details of the project, please refer to Kanyal and Cooper, 2012). Children participating in the study were asked to draw two pictures (actual school and ideal school picture – examples are shown in Figures 7.1A, 7.1B, 7.2A and 7.2B overleaf). The inspiration of using an actual and ideal school picture was taken from Armstrong's (2007) work where she refers to children's school pictures as a useful medium to understand their instructional preferences and learning styles. The instrument, Armstrong (2007) states, can be used effectively with children as young as age five.

Children were asked to draw two separate pictures: picture 1 about their 'actual school experience' and picture 2 about their 'ideal school experience'. In the 'actual school experience' they were advised to draw the day-to-day things that they do in the school/ classroom. In their 'ideal school experience' they were advised to use their imagination and draw the things that they 'would like to see themselves doing in the school'. The drawings, showing their own lives in the classroom/school, were aimed to act as stimuli to elicit narratives about their perceptions of the learning environment (Formosinho and Araújo, 2006). In order to capture the true meaning of drawings, children's narratives were tape recorded whilst they were actively engaged in the process (Robert-Holmes, 2005; Coates and Coates, 2006). Each participating child was briefed on this process beforehand and was given the time to familiarise themselves with the equipment and the researcher.

Both drawings were aimed to be a representation of children's perceptions of their learning environment. In order to represent the learning environment, they were advised to put themselves, their teacher and a friend or two in the drawing. They were encouraged to talk about what each person in their drawing was doing and also, if possible, label the people in their drawing (Armstrong, 2007). These instructions were aimed to facilitate children's imagination, giving their thinking some cognitive structure.

in England and India. A common element, however, is the teacher's authority position which underlines children's common experiences within an education context. The general experiences analysed from the actual school drawings are academically driven and represent a traditional view of the classroom, where the teacher takes the authority position and children attend to instructions (Lodge, 2007; Weber and Mitchell, 1995).

The ideal school drawings, on the other hand, illustrate children's desire to be outside, regardless of the context. The children in the school in India, in addition, referred to some physical well-being factors, such as an adequate arrangement of fans and light. Both sets of drawings highlight the children's common wish to be outside. These imaginary representations remind us that

Here is an example of what children produced in both contexts – the school in England and the school in India:

FIGURE 7.1A Example of 'actual school drawing' by a child in India

The teacher is sitting at the front and my friends and I are in the class. My teacher teaches us. She has punished some children who are standing at the end.

FIGURE 7.1B Example of 'ideal school drawing' by a child in India

In my ideal school there are nice trees, table, fans and my books.

FIGURE 7.2A Example of 'actual school drawing' by a child in England

The teacher is saying 'Now class' in the speech bubble and asking us Maths questions. She asks 'is 3+3=7?' I say 'No', and then I say '6' is my answer. I then ask the teacher if I could go to the toilet. I have drawn my friends Caitlin and Antony in the picture. They are chatting to each other and being a bit naughty. These green things are socks in the classroom. The carpet is all blue. I drew a red chair.

FIGURE 7.2B Example of 'ideal school drawing' by a child in England

In this picture I am playing with my friends Brody, Ollie, Izzy, Ella and Elle. We are playing football together. I am trying to score a goal. There is no teacher in the picture.

children as young as six have knowledge of the symbolic relation of drawings to reality (O'Connor et al., 1981).

To summarise the methodological application of children's drawings as a participatory tool, children were quite comprehensive and confident in narrating their drawings to the researcher(s). They managed to draw contrasting differences between their actual and ideal school experience. This draws us towards the belief that drawings can be used as an effective tool to promote dialogues between young people and their teacher(s) (Lodge, 2007). Drawings therefore can be seen as rendering themselves to a form of text which can be 'read' and understood (Weber and Mitchell, 1996, cited in Lodge, 2007), making them a reliable research instrument in understanding children's everyday experiences.

Their use as a participatory approach to understanding children's views can be achieved if meaning making is shared and mutually discussed amongst the teacher and the children. A record of children's narration of their drawings is therefore important. They can prove to be a powerful medium to enable children to express their views about the learning environment, be it an implicit criticism or a celebration of their teacher's pedagogical practice. Drawings can especially give an opportunity to a child, who is not a profound speaker, to express his/her views. The use of drawings, as a participatory tool, can therefore be argued to enable children to get their voices heard, fulfilling Article 12 of the UNCRC (United Nations, 1989). These voices can be explicit (for example, depicting a traditional classroom view through their actual school drawings) or implicit (indirectly urging to spend more time outside). The tool can also be seen to be efficient enough to be channelising a socially and culturally constructed voice, a voice which is influenced by the cultural tools and contexts in which a child lives. The difference between the English and the Indian drawings is a prime example of this. It is therefore justifiable to state that drawings can sufficiently be used as a participatory tool to provide a socially 'safe space' for the participants to participate freely within various degrees of participation (Bergold and Thomas, 2012), placing emphasis on locally defined perspectives (Cornwall and Jewkes, 1995), which in this case are young children within their learning environments.

SECTION 3
INTERVIEWS: USING INTERVIEWS TO HELP CHILDREN TALK ABOUT THEIR SCHOOL EXPERIENCE

Linda Cooper

Children's participation in research has long been ignored, as their responses are often disregarded as trivial owing to their age and immaturity (Formosinho and Araújo, 2006). Using examples from research with five- and six-year-old children, I argue that children can provide meaningful insights into their own learning environments through the use of interviews or small group discussions. Capturing children's own interpretations of their worlds and acting on their opinions enables children the opportunity to exercise individual agency within their setting, which ultimately leads to a sense of worth and inclusion in their wider peer groups (Kanyal and Cooper, 2012). Brooker (2010) supports the view that adults interpret play and learning differently from children and it is therefore necessary to gain the child's voice in relation to their experiences. It is important for practitioners to listen to all children's preferred voices in their day-to-day context, whether verbal or non-verbal (Flewitt, 2005). However, my focus in this part of the chapter is identifying the benefit derived from the use of speech to prompt both mutual interaction and exchange of ideas between adult and child.

Practitioners who are made aware of both concerns and good practice within a setting, particularly from the children themselves, can address these issues and provide a safer, more stimulating and inclusive learning experience for them (Delamont, 2002; Warren, 2005). To enable this to happen, adults must put their own beliefs and convictions aside and focus on the rights of children to learn 'unfettered' (Brooker, 2010: 43). Furthermore, enabling children to contribute to the decision-making process is not only good practice but it is also their entitlement. Article 12 of the United Nations Convention on the Rights of the Child (respect for the views of the child) asserts that 'When adults are making decisions that affect children, children have the right to say what they think should happen and have their opinions taken into account' (Unicef, 2012).

Interest is growing in the field of capturing children's perspectives in order to adopt a reflexive approach to knowledge construction around children's lives, as well as empowering children to participate as active researchers (Kellett et al., 2004; Formosinho and Araújo, 2006; Canning, 2007). Brooker (2010: 44) argues that adults working with children must always ask 'where are the children in this debate and what do they make of their experiences?' One of the advantages of interviewing children is that it allows for the nuances of face-to-face interaction to be understood with immediacy (Whitehead, 2004). In the case of young children, other methods can be adopted to support the accuracy of the children's responses, such as asking the children to draw their thoughts or take photographs of their environment (Kanyal and Cooper, 2012).

Those who question the engagement of young children in research also suggest that coercion or influence by the inexperienced interviewer can make children complicit in their answers (Krähenbühl and Blades, 2005). Like Krähenbühl and Blades, Formosinho and Araújo (2006) also highlight the importance of thorough rehearsal of the format and style of question as it increases the opportunity for accurate responses. A naturalistic environment for the interview is necessary to provide optimum comfort to the child, reduce the possibility of anxiety and allow the child to speak freely and at will (Kanyal and Cooper, 2012).

Addressing the gap in research into children's own perspectives during the period from pre-school to school (Evans and Fuller, 1998), Mallika Kanyal and

I, from Anglia Ruskin University, carried out a small scale, cross cultural study. This involved twelve children, aged five and six years old, in a school in the East of England, which was replicated in a university campus school in north India (Kanyal and Cooper, 2012).

Three methods were used to collect the data: interviews, children's drawings and photographic evidence. Here I will focus on the findings from the English school only and discuss our use of interviews as one method to capture the voices of children's schooling experience. The earlier section on children's drawings as a method of listening to their voices demonstrated a powerful way of eliciting children's multiple voices. Outlined in Box 7.3 is an example from the same research of using a play telephone as a prop in the interview process with children. It became a useful participatory technique in helping children feel at ease as well as a playful medium for engaging their attention. Discussion revolves around careful choice of words, questions, the use of toys as prompts and the importance of the optimal environment in which to encourage children to share their views.

Permission to carry out the research was given by the school and then informed consent was sought from their parents and children. The children were interviewed in their regular classroom, a safe and known environment for them. Carrying out the research in this naturalistic environment meant that the children welcomed me, even as an unknown outsider, with relative ease, being used to frequent visitors to their space (Denzin and Lincoln, 2008).

The class teacher remained within the large classroom during all interviews with the children, but she was not party to our conversations in order to respect the confidentiality between researcher and child. Whilst the primary aim of the research was to discover the views of the child, it was also important to alleviate any apprehension the class teacher may have perceived, either from the presence of external researchers within the classroom setting or from the responses of the children. Confidentiality and professionalism are crucial here, to reiterate that the findings gathered are to support the children's learning environment and well-being in school. The exercise of encouraging the children to share their viewpoints can be used positively to celebrate good practice within the setting (Kanyal and Cooper, 2012). Any negative comments from the children were not in any way seen as a threat to the teacher's abilities or performance.

In giving consideration to children's comfort and safety, interviewing two children together in friendship pairs is a convenient way to help the child to feel at ease (Whitehead, 2004). Co-operative peer support can potentially lead to copying of answers or one child dominating the conversation, which is cited as a reason not to listen to children's perspectives, but we found no instances of duplicated answers.

It is crucial that the children really feel comfortable and have as much control as possible of the situation during the interview process. Accordingly, a conscious awareness needs to be maintained of the power relations between the adult and child. Adults are viewed as authority figures in the classroom and control the decision whether to include children in a collaborative learning process (Robinson and Kellett, 2004). This highlights the possible tensions when practitioners oppose progressive change, such as the practice of children as partners in learning.

Brooker (2004) and Formosinho and Araújo (2006) suggest that certain preconditions must be created in order to execute successful and valid interviews with children. These preconditions include issues of context in which the interviews are carried out, the number of children interviewed simultaneously, the interview medium used and the number of questions asked. These criteria aim to maximise the children's levels of concentration and to avoid confusion.

Box 7.3 describes the interview process that I carried out with children and a summary of children's responses to the interview questions.

Listening to children's voices is being more widely addressed in early childhood pedagogy (Formosinho and Araújo, 2006). I would argue that the variety and depth of the answers we received suggest children are capable of expressing themselves in a coherent and intelligible way. As such, their opinions are a necessary addition to any decision-making process in an education setting. There are a limited number of ways in which children can perceive their world (Evans and Fuller, 1998) and from three questions we obtained over twenty separate, yet relevant answers regarding the children and their environment. Conversations with and responses from children can inform the practitioner with insights into enhancing the child's learning experience. If the school or setting is willing to positively engage with the answers provided by the children, the opinion of one child may ultimately lead to the possibility of a more responsive learning environment for all children within each setting.

In conclusion, children's participation is easily achievable through shared dialogue. By encouraging children to express their views, by practitioners listening and responding, these conversations can provide a simple yet powerful way of enabling children to be agents of individual choice. The researcher must consider carefully the number of questions used and the way in which these are asked to avoid coercion and to gain, as far as possible, the most accurate responses.

Children's right to be listened to and to have their views taken into account are necessary and an important part of supporting children's learning. In order to really gain insight and understanding into children's opinions and experiences, it is necessary not only to listen to their perspectives, but also to act on the findings. This research has shown techniques that encourage shared participation to elicit children's viewpoints. Through discussion over toy telephones, we were able to engage in a two-way learning process. This is replicable with young children and consideration can be given to the use of other props such as puppets or learning journals. The findings and methods illustrated here support an argument for child friendly, yet informative ways of speaking to children and gaining useful information in order to provide the best play and learning conditions possible.

BOX 7.3: INTERVIEWS WITH CHILDREN

For all interviews, the children were given the choice of a play telephone or a disused mobile telephone. The children each chose a telephone and the interviews were carried out 'over the telephone'. This role play encouraged the children to talk, both in answer to the research questions and in imaginative play. On completion of her interview, one girl immersed herself in play 'birthday party' arrangements 'over the telephone'. Her conversation included a description of the limousine that would take her to London and the friends who would be joining her. She went away to the messy area and 'made' her birthday cake from play dough to show the class and found squares of paper to give out as 'invitations'. The child not only answered the interview questions, but also used our conversation 'over the telephone' to extend her own learning from her birthday party narrative. This example of extended play supports findings that learning through play is most effective when children are immersed in their activities (Canning, 2007).

The children were asked three carefully worded questions: Why do you come to school; what do you like about your school or class; and is there anything at all that you do not like about your school or class? Even with such a small number of questions, we generated a large number of answers. These responses were collected very quickly and importantly for the children, in a fun way.

Why do you come to school?

Answers included responses that affect the children personally, such as liking to come to school to meet their teachers and friends. We also received comments from the children that they needed to come to school in order to improve their future job prospects in adult life. This highlights the imposition of an adult perspective on the child learners and the way that adult views have the ability to impact powerfully upon a child's thinking (Warren, 2005).

What do you like about your school or class?

Activities included symbolic play and sensory-motor activities including the use of materials such as paint or water. Interestingly, these popular activities all included involvement with an adult or peer, highlighting the importance of peer and adult interaction in school life (Robinson and Kellett, 2004).

Is there anything at all that you do not like about your school or class?

Answers included mathematics, physical education, assembly and acts of mild aggression, such as being pushed by other children.

SECTION 4
USING QUESTIONNAIRES WITH CHILDREN

Linda Cooper and Mallika Kanyal

The questionnaire is a commonly used tool in research data collection. It is a method used to amass larger amounts of self-reported data through open ended or closed questions, in a relatively quick and easy way (Coolican, 2009). Its use with children has been less popular as compared to other methods, but researchers have used them successfully by making their format more 'child friendly' (Fargas-Malet et al., 2010), for example using pre-recorded questions played on a personal stereo (Scott, 2000) and using smiley questionnaires (Mortimore et al., 1988).

Questionnaires may have some advantages, for example they can be one of the most economical ways of tapping the views of a sizeable number of children (Hill, 2006); they are relatively quick to administer; and some children may prefer to answer questions through a questionnaire rather than facing an interview situation with a stranger (Fargas-Malet et al., 2010). There is also a likelihood of getting fair representation as the chances of power differentials between children–children and adults–children, which are often realised in group situations, are minimised (Hill, 2006). Questionnaires enable a child's view to be recorded rather than getting an adult imparted response (Robinson and Kellett, 2004). There may also be an advantage of ensuring anonymity, especially by not spreading children's responses which may happen in group or class discussion (Hill, 2006).

Despite these benefits, there are also some issues. First of all, there is comparatively little research on the use of questionnaires with young children (Lewis and Lindsay, 2002) to draw examples and inspirations from. Reasons associated with this could be linked to a low return rate of questionnaires; children's urge to respond to *all* questions, even the ones they do not know the answer to (Fargas-Malet et al., 2010); difficulty of controlling the variables that can affect children's response (Coolican, 2009); challenge of removing the social and institutional bias (Scott, 2000); and finally due to the demand for a certain level of literacy skills (Fargas-Malet et al., 2010).

In order to overcome the literacy related problems with young children (under 8s), which is often cited as the most common issue with the use of questionnaires, researchers, as an alternative, have been working with older children to recite questions to the younger children, especially where the older children take the role of children researchers (see Kellett, 2005). Some have even used tape recorders to allow children to listen to the question, though their responses were given in writing in the form of booklets, answered by children at their own pace (Scott, 2000). Technology has also been used to make the process *fun* and young respondents (as compared to adults) have been found to be happy to answer sensitive questions on a computer-based questionnaire rather than with a pencil or in a face-to-face situation (Kim et al., 2010). In order to ensure a good response rate to questionnaires, some researchers have also included children in the writing process while putting the questionnaire together. Their involvement increases the likelihood of completing and responding to the questionnaire (Lightfoot and Sloper, 2002 and Adams and Ingham, 1998, cited in Hill, 2006) at the same time making it a participatory process.

In order to get our questions right, we first need to consider the variables which often affect the participant's response, making questionnaires an unreliable tool to be used with children (Coolican, 2009). These variables can include the wording of the question, the interpretation of the answer by the adult, the mindset and environment of the participant at the point of answering the questionnaire. These are all important points to consider when working with children. Taking these points in turn, we address possible strategies to work with these potential barriers.

The use of words and pictures

It is vital that the questions asked are simple to understand and the level of literacy is suitable for the participant group. In the case of young children, picture cues can be used. The child can point or mark a cross to pictures and images of their choice. For instance, the question can be asked 'what do you like to eat at snack time?', with an inclusion of images as choice of responses within the question. This allows the children to have agency over their choices and be a co-researcher in discovering the information (Robinson and Kellett, 2004).

It is important that if the questions are written, the child is able to seek help if they have difficulty in understanding the questions. It is vital that the child has an explicit understanding of what the question is asking in order to answer the question fully and without guessing. A question may be obvious for adults but not so clear for a young child, illustrated below through an example:

Question (i): Do you like your classroom environment?

This is a leading question that could be answered with a straight 'yes' or 'no'. Equally, the child might not understand the word 'environment' and guess the answer.

Question (ii): What do you like in your classroom?

Question (iii): Is there anything you do not like about your classroom?

These questions allow the child to expand on their answers by addressing their likes and dislikes and avoid closed questioning.

The mindset and environment of the participant

Children need to be engaged in their activities in order to undertake them with interest and honesty. Asking children to complete a questionnaire just before lunch time or home time will result in rushed and vague responses. A child's concentration will most likely be at its highest in the morning and when the children are alert and willing to be involved in an activity. The child also needs to show their consent, in order that they are undertaking the research without coercion and in agreement to the task they have been set. Lancaster (2006) asserts the need to check with children that as adults we have accurately interpreted their experiences.

'Child friendly' questionnaires

Moving beyond the traditional format of questionnaires, they can also be used in alternate forms to interact with children. We used smiley boxes to record children's consent to participate in our study (for details see Box 7.1), presented to them as an altered form of questionnaire. The use of 'smiley questionnaires' or a similar visual prompt is not a new research tool. Mortimore et al. used the Smiley Attitude Assessment in 1988, and various modifications have been made since. With children, an addition of smiley faces and/or relevant images can make questionnaires a more interesting, yet relevant tool to record responses. For details on the use of smiley questionnaires, please refer to Mortimore et al.'s (1988) study. Further, the work of West and Sammons (1991) could also be explored where they devise a smiley scale to measure children's attitudes towards school. It gives details on the use of a five point scale, represented by five faces, ranging from 'very happy' to 'very sad'. Similar ideas can be adopted and altered to gain insight into children's perceptions through the use of questionnaires.

SECTION 5
USING VISUAL AND AURAL TECHNOLOGY AS TOOLS TO ENHANCE CHILDREN'S PARTICIPATION IN RESEARCH

Rebecca Webster

This section of the chapter explores the use of digital technology and in particular the use of video as a research tool for capturing children's voice. It considers the ways in which video might be used to enhance participatory research and issues for researchers or educators using this rich but complex approach.

Enabling children to be active participants means that children involved in being listened to, should have different types of opportunities to portray their views. Article 13 of the UNCRC (United Nations, 1989) indicates that children should be given the opportunity to respond to issues which impact on their lives through a range of creative mechanisms. Smith (2011: 15) considers that the 'greater the richness of activities and communications that children participate in, the greater will be their competence'. In order to embrace the principles of democratic participation, Clark et al. (2003) suggest that researchers should set aside their agendas and facilitate children's freedom of expression by using a multi-media approach.

Digital technology such as Dictaphones, cameras and video cameras are all tools that enable snap-shots of children's views and perceptions to be captured. Multi-media approaches such as videos, digital photography and video cameras all offer different but potentially valuable ways of capturing pupils' voices and enabling participatory approaches to be developed in research with children.

Video-based methods

Video-based methods of research have become increasingly popular in educational research. This is due to the technical developments, affordability (and thus increased availability) and its perceived power to 'democratise the research process' (Haw and Hatfield, 2011: 8), thus *potentially* enabling participation. Hand held video cameras which are simple to use offer an inclusive approach to research with young children. Robson (2011: 179) suggests that video data may be particularly of value with children as video connects readily to their interests in image making, and their position as 'practised consumers' of interpreting and making meaning from television or video in their everyday lives.

In my own research (Webster, 2010) video has been used as a tool for capturing children's perspectives which aimed to explore what was important in children's lives in order to consider implications for their schooling. Without exception, the children, aged 5–6 years old, who were participants in the research were given the opportunity to use video cameras as a tool for data collection. All of the children were interested in using them and were able to demonstrate their competence by capturing elements of their lives at home and at school. Through a range of researcher-initiated and child-initiated activities the use of video provided opportunities for the children to capture what mattered in their lives as individuals. Issues of privacy, censorship and boundaries were central to many of the discussions held with the children and were prevalent within the video clips recorded in the home environment.

Video has many advantages as a tool for data collection. It may capture situations that could be too intrusive in other formats (Haw and Hadfield, 2011). Although this is an advantage it is important that the 'intrusions' are appropriate and the research is sensitive to the children and families who participate. Ethical issues must be given full consideration throughout the planning and duration of any research with children. Video recordings may offer children the opportunity to show elements of their lives, which might not be otherwise captured through visual or auditory methods. It supports the participation of children who might not be able to communicate their ideas of feelings through traditional research approaches.

Different uses of video in participatory research

The unique nature of capturing moving images, sounds and voices enables the collection of rich data. Exploration of the ways in which video might be used varies between the design and aims of the research. Haw and Hadfield (2011) suggest five categories in which video-based research can be positioned. These are: video as representation; video as an aid to reflection; video that generates participation; video that supports voice and articulation; and finally, video that acts as provocation. These categories are useful when considering research design and the nature of the data to be collected and analysed.

Considering research from a children's rights perspective, video as a tool for generating participation and that supports voice and articulation (Haw and Hadfield, 2011) are both appropriate uses. Also important, from this perspective, is consideration of the analysis processes. Robson (2011) suggests that there is a lack of engagement with children in the analysis and interpretation processes. If we are to be participatory in our data collection methods, then we must also consider the ways in which children can support the analysis of their recordings.

Forman (1999) advocates that video cameras enable children to engage with their own actions in a reflective way. The facility of being able to instantly watch a piece of recorded footage enables the child to move their thinking from beyond the physical and instant action to thinking about what the children have done and why. This enables the children to take an active role in the analysis of the videos and also creates opportunities to think about their learning as well as offering adults insight into understanding the ways in which the children interpret their own actions.

Within my own participatory research (Webster, 2010) conducted with children in school and at home, the participants were given the opportunity to share their video clips with me. Not all children wanted to do this. Those who did opt to discuss their filming were able to add additional and important information which was central to understanding what mattered to them. This was an important stage of the analysis process. Without the children's input there was the potential to 'miss' something which was important to the children or indeed to misinterpret the value of a piece of footage.

Developing competence in using research tools

One of the arguments against the use of video as a research tool is that the equipment such as video cameras may cause 'procedural reactivity', inhibiting participants' behaviours and changing their everyday behaviour and activities (Prosser, 1998). It is important to enable the children the opportunity to become familiar and competent users of the equipment and give them the ownership of the resource, in addition to helping establish the context for the research (Greig et al., 2007). Opportunities to become familiar with the equipment are important, not only for the reasons described above. Through confidence and competence in using the equipment the children begin to understand more fully the 'product' that they create when capturing data, and begin to describe their data to their 'audience'. This 'audience' might be a parent, teacher, peer, researcher or any other intended viewer. This in turn may also help them make valuable and informed decisions about what to capture on camera and what to omit.

The value of children capturing their own data and having some input into the analysis processes helps to address some of the balance of power issues which often feature in research with children. There are opportunities with video, when taking digital photographs and when capturing children's 'voice' on digital Dictaphones, to play back information that has been recorded. In doing so, children are able to 'rehearse' and 'perform' scenes on the video cameras and importantly, choose which data they want to include or delete. The use of such technologies has the potential to enable children's ongoing consent by enabling them to choose the data which is included as part of the research process.

Central in much participatory research is the notion that a shared reflection, which involves children and teachers reflecting and thinking together, can be empowering. Loizou (2011: 44) suggests that practitioners and researchers need to empower children to 'think, reflect and be critical of the indirect imposition of ideas, activities and culture by others', such as adults. This approach supports a rights framework and encourages children to communicate their opinions. Without listening and reflecting, it is difficult to truly understand the value and the relevance of what children tell us. As Underdown and Barlow (2007: 162) state, 'we can only really know "what is best" by tuning into a child's individual preferences and giving these consideration'.

There are many advantages and issues when using digital, visual and aural technology with children to capture children's views on issues which impact on their lives. The use of such methods needs to be given due consideration, be sensitive to the participants' needs and be ethical at every stage of the research. With these commitments in place, there is a wealth of opportunities for rich data to be captured, discussed, analysed and acted upon to enhance provision for children.

SECTION 6
OBSERVATION AS A STRATEGY FOR PARTICIPATION

Paulette Luff

Observation of young children can be traced back to the work of Charles Darwin and his contemporaries. As a research tool, it was employed by members of the Child Study Movement including Granville Stanley Hall and his student Arnold Gesell and, later, by Jean Piaget and others (see Fawcett, 2009 and Papatheodorou and Luff, 2011 for summaries of the history of child observation). At the same time as observation was being developed within the discipline of developmental psychology, pioneers of early childhood education were also advocating its use. Arguably, developmental psychologists used observation as a way of knowing about children whilst educators used observation as a way of getting to know children as people. It is, therefore, the pedagogical uses of observation employed by Maria Montessori, Margaret McMillan and Susan Isaacs that provide some important clues about using observation as a strategy to enable participation. All three of these women stressed the importance of appreciating young children's views and listening to their voices and there is much that present-day observers (both researchers and educators) can learn from their writings.

Maria Montessori (1912) based her method of early education upon understanding and following the child in order to provide personalised learning and teaching activities. She wrote: 'The teacher will note whether or not the child is interested in the object, how he shows his interest, how long he is interested in it, and so on, and she will take care not to force a child's interest in what she is offering' (Montessori, 1967: 107). Margaret McMillan (1919) created her Nursery School as a place to be seen and observed by the surrounding community. Her trainees visited children in their homes to see and understand the social circumstances in which children and their families lived. Likewise, Susan Isaacs (1929) emphasised the keen awareness of young children's perspectives that can be achieved through observation: 'by patient listening to the talk of even little children, and watching what they do, with the one purpose of understanding them, we can imaginatively feel their fears and angers, their bewilderments and triumphs; we can wish their wishes, see their pictures and think their thoughts' (page 165). She did not just attend to those children who responded as a teacher might wish, but 'was just as ready to record and to study the less attractive aspects of their behaviour as the more pleasing' (Isaacs, 1933: 19).

The ideas of these influential women are echoed in the present-day principle that 'good information about childhood must start from children's experience' (Mayall, 2000: 121). Thoughtful watching of children, in order to understand their perspectives and interests and plan their care and education, is vital. For example, when implementing the Early Years Foundation Stage curriculum (DfE, 2012; Early Education, 2012) practitioners working with children from birth to age five years, in England, use observation as a means to get to know each unique child, to create positive relationships with children and families, to provide suitable enabling environments and to recognise, support and promote children's development and learning.

Since the publication and ratification of the UN Convention on the Rights of the Child (United Nations, 1989), arguments for open-minded, responsive observation (aimed at understanding and appreciating children's lives and achievements and acting to promote their care and extend their learning) have been framed in terms of respecting and upholding children's rights (for example, Nutbrown 1996; Santer and Griffiths, 2007). Article 12 (United Nations, 1989) concerns the child's right to express views on matters concerning them, which has prompted specific attempts to listen to children's voices and viewpoints (for example, MacNaughton et al., 2003; Dahl and Aubrey, 2005; Lancaster and Kirby, 2010). Observation of children can be seen as a strategy for listening, particularly when children cannot verbalise their views (Elfer, 2005; Palaiologou, 2008) and may provide a means for adults to understand what children are trying to say and to support them in expressing their views.

Clark et al. (2005) offer a critical examination of approaches to listening to young children in early childhood services. Their book includes eight examples of research and practice, from six European countries, all of which contain elements of observation and reveal its importance as a means of attending to and incorporating children's views when improving their care and education. The methods of observation employed vary but are characterised by participatory roles for the adult observers and for children. Within the Mosaic approach, for example, adults' accounts, based upon qualitative observations, provide part of a repertoire of ways of seeing provision from the children's points of view (Clark, 2005). Warming (2005) aims to understand children's perspectives through the active adoption of a 'least adult role' (following Corsaro, 1985). In playing alongside the children she gains an appreciation of their lives in the kindergarten and also reveals how some children are skilled in keeping themselves hidden from adults' sight.

These children who keep themselves hidden from view raise some doubts about the use of observation as a way of listening to children. Silin (2005: 84) questions the 'uncensored celebration of voice', as privileging certain social and cultural groups, and asks: 'What if we considered the ability to remain still as a critical social skill and silence an essential aspect of our humanity?' Svenning (2009), too, wonders if we are listening in ways that are good enough, and showing sensitivity towards children's potential embarrassment at their behaviours being recorded, recounted and discussed. Thus practitioners and researchers should observe and document with caution and respect.

If we uphold a view of the child as a person with rights and agency then he or she should, as far as possible, have a say in what is observed and documented and have a role in directing research and educational activities (Alderson, 2008; Palaiologou, 2008). The 'Learning Stories' approach to assessment, within Aotearoa New Zealand's Te Whāriki curriculum, offers a good example of children's voices being heard within the observation process (Carr, 2001; Carr and Lee, 2012). The Kei Tua o te Pae exemplars from the New Zealand Ministry of Education (2009) demonstrate how children's stories are captured and documented using written observations and other means, such as their artwork or digital photographs. Teachers, children and parents all contribute to and interpret the learning story in order to review what has been attained and make decisions about future learning goals. The example here (Box 7.4), written by Opeyemi Osadiya, an MA Early Childhood Studies student at Anglia Ruskin University, shows how a 'Learning Stories' approach is adopted and analysed to record the achievements of a 3.5-year-old child. It shows the observer's and parents' perspective and also includes the child's voice.

BOX 7.4: LEARNING STORY EXAMPLE

M's musical performance

A 'Learning Stories' child: M.

Age: 3 years and 4 months – at home with 3 adults.

M came into the living room with his toy guitar, microphone and stand. He started to set them up in the living room. When I asked him: 'what are you doing, M?' he answered: 'I'm setting up my music stand and I'm going to sing a song for you'.

He finished setting up his stand, and he started singing 'Twinkle, twinkle, little star, how I wonder what you are . . .' We all clapped for him at the end. When we asked him if he would like to do it again, he happily obliged us.

Short-term review and what next?

M displayed genuine interest in his singing. He sang with confidence and mimicked professional singers on TV. M was also interested in playing the guitar. Maybe M would like to be a performer when he grows older. This is a good example of M's involvement with something of interest to him – which in this case is music. M can be encouraged to be more involved in playing a variety of musical instruments and attend dance classes.

What aspects of noticing, recognising and responding to learning in the arts does this assessment exemplify?

When M was getting ready for his song, the three adults with him encouraged him to carry on with setting up his music stand as well as making sure that he was safe from the plastic wires. The adults all listened attentively as he sang and gave him a round of applause when he finished. He was also encouraged to sing his song again with praises from all the adults.

What does this assessment tell us about learning in the arts (using a Te Whāriki lens)?

M demonstrated several learning dispositions throughout this observation. He expressed himself by setting up his music stand and singing a much loved song very clearly. M played the guitar and sang to express his feelings. However, we were not sure if he would be able to sing in front of his peers in pre-school. When he was asked to sing the song again, M had no difficulty in doing this and even received the applause, with a flourishing bow.

How does this assessment exemplify developing competence in the arts?

M showed through his performance that he was able to draw on his previous experiences of watching 'X Factor' shows or other musical performances in the ways in which he set up his instruments, held his guitar and performed in front of a 'live' audience. He did this very well and he moved and danced to the music as well. He ended with a bow to the audience (us) when we clapped for him. He is learning the conventions of performing on stage.

Mother's voice

'M likes to sing and makes us laugh so much with his songs. He wouldn't leave us alone until he has got everybody's attention. He really knows what he wants and I think he will become a singer in the future.'

Analysis of the 'Learning Stories' approach to child observation

My observation of M's musical performance has enabled me to place value on his developing competence in the arts. His initiation of the activity showed his involvement with something that was of interest to him. This emphasises the view of the child as a competent learner. There was provision of musical toys and encouragement from his family as he performed. The learning story has also been supported by photograph(s) of the child as he performed his musical experience. This resonates with Rogoff et al.'s (1993, cited in Woodhead, 2006) elaboration of 'guided participation' as a framework for examining the way children are initiated into cognitive and social skills perceived as relevant to their community. This approach to observation and documentation has also been described as the creation of developmental narratives for and about children as it not only captures children's learning but also offers opportunity to revisit the evidence, thus providing feedback to learners as well as enabling educators to reflect upon and develop their pedagogy (Carr, 2001; Van Oers, 2003).

'Learning Stories' provides a good example of observation conducted with respect for children's rights. Anne Smith (2007) points out that this model of observational assessment offers opportunities for children to: 'share meaning and power with adults (teachers and family members), have their voices heard and acted on, develop agency through having the opportunity to take initiative and play responsible roles, and have their strengths and interests respected.' Kjørholt (2005) warns, however, that following a 'rights-based' approach may lead to some superficial ideas and practices when attempting to listen to children; and an over-emphasis upon the child as a rational, autonomous and competent being, which risks neglect of the child's need for sensitive, supportive care. She speaks of the importance of adults having sensitivity and listening to children's unspoken words, and highlights the need for observant attention to body language.

Subtle and sensitive use of observation, as a way of relating to children and promoting their emotional well-being, can be achieved through the close observation of children as pioneered by Esther Bick (1964). This approach, designed for use in the training of psycho-therapists, has been used in the continuing professional development of social workers (Trowell and Miles, 1991) and, more recently, for early years practitioners (Elfer, 2005). It usually involves weekly one-hour visits to a family home in order to follow the development of a baby or very young child throughout a year of their life. The approach to observation is challenging, as the observer aims to be neutral and non-participant yet fully tuned-in to the infant's feelings. No notes are taken but very close attention is paid to the body language of the infant and the features of any interaction between the child and parents, particularly the mother. A detailed account of the session is written up in which, as far as possible, the complete sequence of events is recalled and described. The observation accounts are somewhat different from the objective, factual, narrative records which observers are often encouraged to aim for. They have a distinct emotional quality and incorporate both description and an introspective response from the observer, reflecting upon her own feelings whilst observing. The excerpt below (Box 7.5) is from an observation written by Opeyemi Osadiya, an MA Early Childhood Studies student, experimenting with this technique for the first time.

The extent to which close observation brings the observer in touch with the perspective of the child and parent is evident from this example. Another strategy that can foster empathy with the child is to attempt to gain an appreciation of his or her point of view through recording a narrative observation in the first-person, from the child's perspective. Alice Paige-Smith and Jonathan Rix (2011) used this method of observation as part of their ethnographic research to understand the processes of early interventions with two young children with Down syndrome and their families. It is never entirely possible for the adult to enter into the mind of the child and to provide a genuine account of the child's thoughts but, as in the use of close observation (above), the act of focusing on the child and attempting to decentre and to see the world from a different angle may aid the adult observer in getting closer to the child's experiences and so

BOX 7.5: CLOSE OBSERVATION EXAMPLE

The child, male, is eight months old. The mother and the child are visiting another family. When they arrive, the mother is holding the baby in her arms while the baby's older sibling tags along. The baby appears contented. Mother sits down and puts baby on her lap. Baby keeps looking at mother's face, but mother chats to other people. Baby touches mother's face and she looks at him and smiles. Baby smiles back. Baby keeps touching mother to get her attention and he seems satisfied anytime he gets her attention. Mother is given a drink and the baby looks on. She puts down the cup and continues to play with baby. Mother and baby continue to look at each other and smile at each other every now and then. Mother frequently talks to the baby who would respond with smiles and a few noises.

Baby now begins to fret and mother asks him to stop. Baby stops for a few minutes and then starts fretting again and kicks his legs. He soon begins to cry and the mother now says: 'Ah ha! You need food now, don't you?' She looks in her bag and brings out a bottle full of milk. Baby stops fretting and quietens as soon as he sees the bottle. Mother begins to feed the baby while continuing talking with the people around her.

After a short while, baby's older sibling, a girl, of about 3 years, needed to go to toilet and asks if the mother could take her. Mother removes the bottle from baby's mouth and attempts to stand up, but baby gives a louder wail and mother appears confused. Seeing mother's confusion, another adult now asks mother if she could help hold and feed the baby while the mother takes older sibling to the toilet. Mother now hands the baby to another adult and quickly takes older sibling to the toilet. Baby cries for a while and refuses to take bottle from the other adult. After much coaxing from the adult, the baby continues feeding but does so with his eyes tightly shut. Baby finishes the milk before the mother comes back but still keeps his eyes tightly shut and refuses to look at the other adult and only opens his eyes when he hears his mother's voice. The adult now hands him back to her. He now appears settled and begins to play with his mother again.

identifying with and understanding the child. The following example (Box 7.6), as observed and evidenced by Amal Hussein, an MA Early Childhood Studies student at Anglia Ruskin University, shows how actions that could be interpreted as negative behaviour are understood when explaining events and motivations as if the child were narrating.

This section about observation has offered clues for ways in which observations can be carried out in ways that recognise children as participants in learning and research. Rather than the adult taking a role as a detached and scientific observer, researchers or educators may try these techniques in order to see in ways that take account of the child's perspective and offer greater opportunities for participation.

BOX 7.6: OBSERVATION WRITTEN FROM THE CHILD'S VIEWPOINT

Trip to Home Bargains store

My name is Maher and I am two years old. My grandparents, my mum and I have come to a very big store. On our way to the store it rained, 'drop, drop, drop'. Grand-dad said that this rain was not expected. When we arrived at the store, everyone got out of the car and so did I. My mum held my hand while going into the store but I wanted my grand-dad, who was still far behind. I don't know what he is doing. 'Grand-dad, Grand-dad, Grand-dad' . . . Mum tells me that grand-dad is going to come, 'Let us go in as it is raining'. 'Mum I want grand-dad', I keep telling her but she doesn't understand, also, I like the feel of the rain on my face. Finally, grand-dad comes and he gets the trolley. Here, as always, they are trying to put me in that trolley. I don't want to go in, I want to have my freedom so that I can get what I want from those shelves; so I cry and I scream in my loudest and I make myself static, ahaa, you cannot put me in that trolley, yeah I win. Now mum and grandma want me to hold their hand but I don't want to. Here I set my hands free, let me get that Thomas the Engine in the pack, choo choo choo . . . Grandma asks my mum what is in the pack and mum tells her that it is a bath soap and bath toys. So grandma tells me that they will get me something else as Thomas the Train Engine is not something good. I am thinking, it is a toy and I can play with it, and even if it is not a toy, I still want it, it is Thomas the Engine after all. Again they want me to hold their hand, so they tell me that the man will take me away if I don't listen to them. They think I don't understand, they want to inhibit my freedom, but I am clever, I hold their hand but soon I will set myself free. Here is a Hello Kitty piano, ting tin trin . . . This is fun, let me get a couple of them and put them in the trolley . . .

Summary and conclusion

The chapter gives a brief outline of participatory research and various approaches used in participatory research. Different methods, for example drawings, interviews, questionnaires, video cameras and observations, are discussed as participatory research methods, in relation to doing research with young children. Examples from practice and research show how these methods could be used effectively to promote children's participation, and therefore their rights, in an education and care context.

Points to consider and questions to ask yourself

- In what ways do you encourage children to discuss their concerns or opinions about their surroundings and interests? How do you respond to their suggestions? What impact does this make on your relationship with children?

- What methods can you employ to include children as research participants? How can you obtain and record their consent?
- What methods can you employ to 'listen' to the views of the 'youngest'? How can you incorporate these views into your planning and work?

References

Alderson, P. 2008. *Young Children's Rights: Exploring Beliefs, Principles and Practice* (2nd edn). London: Jessica Kingsley Publishers.

Anning, A. and Ring, K. 2004. *Making Sense of Children's Drawings*. Maidenhead: Open University Press.

Armstrong D. 2007. Classroom visions: efficient and effective ways to differentiate education. [Online]. Available at http://www.classroomvisions.com/ClassroomVisions/Classroom Visions_main.html. Accessed January 10, 2009.

Bergold, J. and Thomas, S. 2012. Participatory research methods: a methodological approach in motion. *FQS Forum: Qualitative Social Research*, 13 (1).

Bick, E. 1964. Notes on infant observation in psychoanalytic training. *International Journal of Psychoanalysis*, 45: 558–566.

Bonoti, F., Plousia, M. and Fotini, G. 2003. Graphic indicators of pedagogic style in Greek children's drawings. *Perceptual and Motor Skills*, 97: 195–206.

Bragg, S. (2007). 'Student voice' and governmetality: the production of enterprising subjects? *Discourse: Studies in the Cultural Politics of Education*, 28 (3): 343–358.

Brooker, L. 2004. Interviewing children, in G. MacNaughton, S. Rolfe and I. Siraj-Blatchford (eds). *Doing Early Childhood Research: International Perspectives on Theory and Practice*. Buckingham: Open University Press.

Brooker, L. 2010. Learning to play or playing to learn? Children's participation in the cultures of homes and settings, in L. Brooker and S. Edwards (eds). *Engaging Play*. Berkshire: Open University Press.

Campbell, F., Beasley, L., Eland, J. and Rumpus, A. 2007. Hearing the student voice: promoting and encouraging the effective use of the student voice to enhance professional development in learning, teaching and assessment within higher education. ESCalate (Education Subject Centre of the Higher Education Academy), Corp creator. [Online]. Available at http://dera.ioe.ac.uk/13053/. Accessed September 28, 2012.

Canning, N. 2007. Children's empowerment in play. *European Early Childhood Education Research Journal*, 15 (2): 227–236.

Carr, M. 2001. *Assessment in Early Childhood Settings: Learning Stories*. London: Paul Chapman Publishing.

Carr, M. and Lee, W. 2012. *Learning Stories: Constructing Learner Identities in Early Education*. London: Sage.

Clark, A. 2005. Ways of seeing: using the Mosaic approach to listen to young children's perspectives, in A. Clark, A. T. Kjørholt and P. Moss (eds). *Beyond Listening*. Bristol: The Policy Press.

Clark, A. 2010. *Transforming Children's Spaces: Children's and Adults' Participation in Designing Learning Environments*. London: Routledge.

Clark, A. and Moss, P. 2006. *Listening to Young Children: The Mosaic Approach*. London: National Children's Bureau.

Clark, A., Kjørholt, A. T. and Moss, P. 2005. *Beyond Listening: Children's Perspectives on Early Childhood Services*. Bristol: The Policy Press.

Clark, A., McQuail, S. and Moss, P. 2003. Exploring the field of listening to and consulting with young children. *Research Report* 445. London: Department for Education and Skills.

Coates, E. and Coates, A. 2006. Young children talking and drawing. *International Journal of Early Years Education*, 14 (3): 221–241.

Cohen, L., Manion, L. and Morrison, K. 2011. The nature of enquiry, in *Research Methods in Education* (7th edn). Abingdon: Routledge.

Coolican, H. 2009. *Research Methods and Statistics in Psychology* (5th edn). London: Hodder Education.

Cornwall, A. and Jewkes, R. 1995. What is participatory research? *Social Science and Medicine*, 41 (12): 1667–1676.

Corsaro, W. 1985. *Friendship and Peer Culture in the Early Years*. Norwood, NJ: Ablex.

Crivello, G., Camfield, L. and Woodhead, M. 2009. How can children tell us about their wellbeing? Exploring the potential of participatory research approaches within young lives. *Social Indicators Research*, 90 (1): 51–72.

Dahl, S. and Aubrey, C. 2005. Children's views: what the children of bright eyes nursery think about the play and learning opportunities available in their setting. University of Warwick: Childhood Research Unit. [Online]. Available at http://www.ness.bbk.ac.uk/support/local-evaluation-findings/documents/1312.pdf. Accessed January 13, 2013.

Delamont, S. 2002. *Fieldwork in Educational Settings: Methods, Pitfalls and Perspectives* (2nd edn). London: Routledge.

Denzin, N. K. and Lincoln, Y. S. (eds). 2008. *Collecting and Interpreting Qualitative Materials* (3rd edn). London: Sage.

DfE (Department for Education). 2012. Statutory Framework for the Early Years Foundation Stage. [Online]. Available at https://www.education.gov.uk/publications/standard/All Publications/Page1/DFE-00023-2012. Accessed January 13, 2013.

Early Education. 2012. Development matters in the Early Years Foundation Stage EYFS. [Online]. Available at https://www.education.gov.uk/publications/standard/publication Detail/Page1/DEVELOPMENT-MATTERS. Accessed January 13, 2013.

Elfer, P. 2005. Observation matters, in L. Abbott and A. Langston (eds). *Birth to Three Matters*. Maidenhead: Open University Press.

Evans, P. and Fuller, M. 1998. Children's perceptions of their nursery education. *International Journal of Early Years Education*, 6 (1): 59–64.

Fargas-Malet, M., McSherry, D., Larkin, E. and Robinson, C. 2010. Research with children: methodological issues and innovative techniques. *Journal of Early Childhood Research*, 8 (2): 175–192.

Fawcett, M. 2009. *Learning through Child Observation* (2nd edn). London: Jessica Kingsley Publishers.

Flewitt, R. 2005. Is every child's voice heard? Researching the different ways 3-year-old children communicate and make meaning at home and in a pre-school playgroup. *Early Years*, 25 (3): 207–222.

Forman, G. 1999. *Instant Video Revisiting: The Video Camera as a 'Tool of the Mind' for Young Children*. ERIC Clearinghouse.

Formosinho, J. and Araújo, S. B. 2006. Listening to children as a way to reconstruct knowledge about children: some methodological implications. *European Early Childhood Education Research Journal*, 14 (1): 21–31.

Gallacher, L. A. and Gallagher, M. 2008. Methodological immaturity in childhood research? Thinking through participatory methods. *Childhood*, 15 (4): 499–516.

Gouin, R. R., Cocq, K. and McGavin, S. 2011. Feminist participatory research in a social justice organisation. *Action Research*, 9 (3): 261–281.

Greig, A., Taylor, J. and Mackay, T. 2007. *Doing Research with Children* (2nd edn). London: Sage.

Grey, C. and Winter, E. 2011. The ethics of participatory research involving young children with special needs, in D. Harcourt, B. Perry and T. Waller (eds). *Researching Young Children's Perspectives*. London: Routledge.

Haw, K. and Hadfield, M. 2011. *Video in Social Science Research: Functions and Forms*. London and New York: Routledge/Taylor & Francis Group.

Hill, M. 2006. Children's voices on ways of having a voice: children's and young people's perspectives on methods used in research and consultation. *Childhood*, 13 (1): 69–89.

Holland, S., Renold, E., Ross, N. J. and Hillman, A. 2010. Power, agency and participatory agendas: a critical exploration of young people's engagement in participative qualitative research. *Childhood*, 17 (3): 360–375.

Isaacs, S. 1929. *The Nursery Years*. London: Routledge and Kegan Paul.

Isaacs, S. 1933. *Social Development in Young Children*. London: Routledge and Kegan Paul.

Kanyal, M. 2012. Children's perceptions of their school experience, in B. Boufoy-Bastick (ed.). *The International Handbook of Cultures of Teacher Education: Comparative International Issues in Curriculum and Pedagogy*. Strasbourg, France: Analytrics.

Kanyal, M. and Cooper, L. 2012. Young children's perceptions of their classroom environment: perspectives from England and India, in T. Papatheodorou and J. Moyles (eds). *Cross-cultural Perspectives on Early Childhood*. London: Sage.

Kellett, M. 2005. *Children as Active Researchers: A New Research Paradigm for the 21st Century?* London: ESRC.

Kellett, M. 2010. Small shoes, big steps! Empowering children as active researchers. *American Journal of Community Psychology*, 46: 195–203.

Kellett, M., Forrest, R., Dent, N. and Ward, S. 2004. 'Just teach us the skills please, we'll do the rest': empowering ten-year-olds as active researchers. *Children and Society*, 18: 329–343.

Kendrick, M. and McKay, R. 2004. Drawings as an alternative way of understanding young children's constructions of literacy. *Journal of Early Childhood Literacy*, 4 (1): 109–128.

Kim, J., Kang, J., Kim, S., Smith, T. W., Son, J. and Berktold, J. 2010. Comparison between self-administered questionnaire and computer-assisted self-interview for supplemental survey nonresponse. *Field Methods*, 22 (1): 57–69.

Kjørholt, A. T. 2005. The competent child and the right to be oneself: reflections on children as fellow citizens in an early childhood centre, in A. Clark, A. T. Kjørholt and P. Moss (eds). *Beyond Listening*. Bristol: The Policy Press.

Komulainen, S. 2007. The ambiguity of the child's 'voice' in social research. *Childhood*, 14 (1): 11–28.

Krähenbühl, S. and Blades, M. 2005. The effect of interviewing techniques on young children's responses to questions. *Child: Care, Health and Development*, 32 (3): 321–331.

Lancaster, Y. P. 2006. Listening to young children: respecting the voice of the child, in G. Pugh and B. Duffy (eds). *Contemporary Issues in the Early Years* (4th edn). London: Sage.

Lancaster, Y. P. and Kirby, P. on behalf of Coram, 2010. *Listening to Young Children* (2nd edn). Maidenhead: Open University Press/Coram Family.

Lewis, A. and Lindsay, G. (eds). 2002. *Researching Children's Perspectives*. Buckingham: Open University Press.

Lodge, C. 2007. Regarding learning: children's drawings of learning in the classroom. *Learning Environment Research*, 10: 145–156.

Loizou, E. 2011. Empowering aspects of transition from kindergarten to first grade through children's voices. *Early Years*, 31 (1): 43–55.

MacNaughton, G., Smith, K. and Lawrence, H. ACT Children's Services Branch, 2003. *Hearing Young Children's Voices*. Parkville, VIC: University of Melbourne, Centre for Equity and Innovation in Early Childhood.

Mayall, B. 2000. Conversations with children: working with generational issues, in P. Christensen and A. James (eds). *Research with Children*. London: Routledge Falmer.

McIntyre, A. 2008. *Participatory Action Research*. London: Sage.

McMillan, M. 1919. *The Nursery School*. London: Dent.

Minkler, M. 2004. Ethical challenges for the 'outside' researcher in community-based participatory research. *Health Education and Behavior*, 31 (6): 684–697.

Montessori, M. 1912. *The Montessori Method* (translated by A. E. George). New York: Frederick A. Stokes Company. [Online]. Available at http://web.archive.org/web/20050207205651/www.moteaco.com/method/method.html. Accessed January 13, 2013.

Montessori, M. 1967. *The Absorbent Mind*. New York: Henry Holt.

Morrow, V. and Richards, M. 1996. The ethics of social research with children: an overview. *Children and Society*, 10 (2): 90–105.

Mortimore, P., Sammons, P., Stoll, L., Lewis, D. and Ecob, R. 1988. *School Matters: The Junior Years*. Somerset: Open Books.

New Zealand Ministry of Education. 2009. Kei Tua o te Pae/Assessment for Learning. [Online]. Available at http://www.educate.ece.govt.nz/learning/curriculumAndLearning/Assessmentforlearning/KeiTuaotePae.aspx. Accessed January 13, 2013.

Nutbrown, C. 1996. *Respectful Educators – Capable Learners: Children's Rights and Early Education*. London: Paul Chapman Publishing.

O'Connor, J., Beilin, H. and Kose, G. 1981. Children's belief in photographic fidelity. *Developmental Psychology*, 17 (6): 859–865.

Paige-Smith, A. and Rix, J. 2011. Researching early intervention and young children's perspectives – developing and using a 'listening to children approach'. *British Journal of Special Education*, 38 (1): 27–36.

Palaiologou, I. 2008. *Childhood Observation*. Exeter: Learning Matters.

Pant, M. n.d. Participatory research. [Online]. Available at http://www.unesco.org/pv_obj_cache/pv_obj_id_8A4DA2D14C7705777AD77C0F25AF56E533F60100/filename/unit_08.pdf. Accessed October 8, 2012.

Papatheodorou, T. and Luff, P. with Gill, J. 2011. *Child Observation for Learning and Research*. Harlow: Pearson.

Pascal, C. and Bertram, T. 2009. Listening to young citizens: the struggle to make real a participatory paradigm in research with young children. *European Early Childhood Education Research Journal*, 17 (2): 249–262.

Prosser, J. 1998. The status of image-based research, in J. Prosser (ed.). *Image-based Research: A Sourcebook for Qualitative Researchers*. London: Falmer Press.

Prout, A., 2001. Representing children: reflections on the children 5–16 programme. *Children and Society*, 15: 193–201.

Punch, K. F. 2011. Theory and method in education research, in *Introduction to Research Methods in Education*. London: Sage.

Riet, M. V. D. 2008. Participatory research and the philosophy of social science: beyond the moral imperative. *Qualitative Inquiry*, 14: 546.

Robert-Holmes, G. 2005. *Doing Your Early Years Research Project: A Step by Step Guide*. London: Paul Chapman.

Robinson, C. and Kellett, M. 2004. Power, in S. Fraser, V. Lewis, S. Ding, M. Kellett and C. Robinson (eds). *Doing Research with Children and Young People*. London: Sage.

Robson, S. 2011. Producing and using video with young children: a case study of ethical questions and practical consequences, in D. Harcourt, B. Perry and T. Waller (eds). *Researching Young Children's Perspectives*. London: Routledge.

Rogoff, B., Mistry, J., Göncü, A. and Mosier, C. 1993. Guided Participation in Cultural Activity by Toddlers and Caregivers. *Monographs of the Society for Research in Child Development*. Serial no. 236, 58 (8): 1–179.

Santer, J. and Griffiths, C. 2007. *Free Play in Early Childhood: A Literature Review*. London: National Children's Bureau.

Scott, J. 2000. Children as respondents: the challenge for quantitative methods, in P. M. Christensen and A. James (eds). *Research with Children: Perspectives and Practices*. London: Falmer Press.

Seale, J. 2010. Doing student voice work in Higher Education: an exploration of the value of participatory methods. *British Educational Research Journal*, 36 (6): 995–1015.

Silin, J. G. 2005. Silence, voice and pedagogy, in N. Yelland (ed.). *Critical Issues in Early Childhood Education*. Maidenhead: Open University Press.

Smith, A. 2007. Children's rights and early childhood education. *Australasian Journal of Early Childhood*, 32 (3), September 2007. [Online]. Available at http://www.earlychildhood australia.org.au/australian_journal_of_early_childhood/ajec_index_abstracts/childrens_rights_and_early_childhood_education.html. Accessed January 13, 2013.

Smith, A. B. 2011. Respecting children's rights and agency, in D. Harcourt, B. Perry and T. Waller (eds). *Researching Young Children's Perspectives*. London: Routledge.

Spyrou, S. 2011. The limits of children's voices: from authenticity to critical, reflexive representation. *Childhood*, 18 (2): 151–165.

Svenning, B. 2009. Approaching the youngest children in day care centres – opportunities, rights and ethics in relation to participation and choice in documentation processes. Poster presented to the 19th European Early Childhood Educational Research Association Annual Conference, Diversities in Early Childhood Education, Strasbourg, 27th–29th August.

The Open University, Children's Research Centre. [Online]. Available at http://www8.open.ac.uk/researchprojects/childrens-research-centre/. Accessed December 15, 2012.

Thomas, N. and O'Kane, C. 1998. The ethics of participatory research with children. *Children and Society*, 12: 336–348.

Tickle, L. 1999. Teacher self appraisal and appraisal of self, in R. P. Lipka and T. M. Brinthaupt (eds). *The Role of Self in Teacher Development*. Albany: State University of New York Press. [Online]. Available at http://site.ebrary.com/lib/anglia/docDetail.action?docID=10039028. Accessed December 18, 2011.

Trowell, J. and Miles, G. 1991. The contribution of observation training to professional development in social work. *Journal of Social Work Practice*, 5 (1): 51–60.

Underdown, A. and Barlow, J. 2006. Listening to young children, in A. Underdown, *Young Children's Health and Well-being*. Berkshire: OU Press McGraw Hill.

Unicef. 2012. Fact sheet: a summary of the rights under the convention on the rights of the child. [Online]. Available at http://www.unicef.org. Accessed February 8, 2012.

United Nations. 1989. Convention on the Rights of the Child. [Online]. Available at http://www2.ohchr.org/english/law/crc.htm. Accessed January 13, 2013.

Van Oers, B. 2003. Learning resources in the context of play: promoting effective learning in early childhood. *European Early Childhood Education Research Journal*, 11 (1): 7–26.

Veale, A. 2005. Creative methodologies in participatory research with children, in S. Greene and D. Hogan (eds). 2005. *Researching Children's Experience: Approaches and Methods*. London: Sage.

Walker, K. 2007. Children and their purple crayons: understanding their worlds through their drawings. [Online]. Available at http://www.freepatentsonline.com/article/Childhood-Education/172907417.html. Accessed January 10, 2012.

Waller, T. and Bitou, A. 2011. Research *with* children: three challenges for participatory research in early childhood. *European Early Childhood Education Research Journal*, 19 (1): 5–20.

Warming, H. 2005. Participant observation: a way to learn about children's perspectives, in A. Clark, A. T. Kjørholt and P. Moss (eds). *Beyond Listening*. Bristol: Policy Press.

Warren, S. 2005. Photography and voice in critical qualitative management research. *Accounting, Auditing and Accountability Journal*, 18: 861–882.

Weber, S. and Mitchell, C. 1995. 'That's funny, you don't look like a teacher': interrogating images and identity in popular culture. Abingdon: Routledge Falmer. [Online].

Available at http://site.ebrary.com/lib/anglia/Doc?id=10058250&ppg=17. Accessed February 10, 2010.

Webster, R. 2010. Listening to and learning from children's perspectives, in J. Moyles (ed.). *Thinking about Play: Developing a Reflective Approach*. Berkshire: Open University Press.

West, A. and Sammons, P. 1991. *The Measurement of Children's Attitudes towards School: The Use of the Smiley Scale*. London: Centre for Educational Research, London School of Economics and Political Science.

Whitehead, M. R. 2004. *Language and Literacy in the Early Years* (3rd edn). London: Sage.

Wimpenny, K. 2010. Participatory action research: an integrated approach towards practice development, in M. Savin-Baden and C. H. Major (eds). *New Approaches to Qualitative Research: Wisdom and Uncertainty*. London: Routledge.

Woodhead, M. 2006. *Changing Perspectives on Early Childhood: Theory, Research and Policy*. Paper commissioned for the Education For All – Global Monitoring Report 2007, Strong foundations: early childhood care and education.

Terminology explained

Action research: Action research is a form of research approach that professionals undertake to improve conditions and practices in a range of (work) contexts, including education. It can be done to improve one's own practice, which in turn can enhance the conditions of a working environment. It involves planning, action and reflection cycle and focuses on bringing about change in specific contexts.

Anti-positivist paradigm: Anti-positivist paradigm originated as a critique of the positivist research paradigm and argued that positivist methodology is not sufficient to help research complex human relations and cultural phenomena. It studies in depth human and cultural processes, with relatively smaller group sizes. The methods used in such researches are more open and allow researchers to engage in much more depth with respondents as compared to the positivist research.

Feminist researchers: A group of female researchers who do research *on* women, *for* women, with a prime aim of female emancipation from the malestream patriarchal society. The foundation of feminist work, like Paulo Freire's and Fals-Borda's, is in critical theory that believes in the emancipatory philosophy, especially of the marginalised. Beyond its emancipatory work, feminist researchers' work is guided by sound research methodologies, producing valuable and high quality research findings.

Objective methodology: A methodology used in positivist research, which relies heavily on experimental and manipulative methods. It follows a scientific approach to understanding (social) reality and enables the researcher to study a large number of respondents. The methods used are measurable and allow for the quantifying and generalising of objective reality.

Orlando Fals-Borda: Orlando Fals-Borda is one of the founders and leading theorists and practitioners of participatory action research (PAR). He connected (critical emancipatory) action research and participatory research as 'PAR', constructing a more humane paradigm in social sciences where marginalised communities can themselves get involved in addressing their problems by engaging with research. His work, like Paulo Freire's, is linked with the empowerment of the marginalised by using participatory action research methodologies.

Paulo Freire: Paulo Freire's work is usually associated with the critical theory perspective where he argues for the empowerment of the 'less powerful'. He puts forward a pedagogy of the oppressed where he strongly critiques the traditional views of the 'more powerful', for example the teachers, who impose their knowledge and beliefs on their clients, the students. He instead argues for a place for critical reflection on the part of the 'subjects' in order to bring about any individual and social change, especially to counter the 'colonial' approaches to knowledge construction within oppressed communities.

Positivist research: A positivist research approach is based on the knowledge that reality can be observed and described from an objective viewpoint. Researches that are grounded in the positivist paradigm use quantitative methods of data collection and analysis, which can be observed and measured objectively.

Qualitative methods: The methods used in research that enable researchers' direct interaction with individuals on a one-to-one or a group basis. The information collected could be from a small sample, but offers rich and deep insight into the phenomenon under study. Some of the qualitative methods are individual interviews, focus groups, observation and action research.

Quantitative measures: The measures used in quantitative researches that are numeric in nature and allow statistical analysis of the data. Some examples of quantitative measures are frequency tables, percentages and averages.

Index

Note: Page numbers followed by 'f' refer to figures and followed by 't' refer to tables.

M

N

O

P

V

W